Too often, we separate our private spiritual lives from h
their typical friendly and accessible style, Jeremy and Monica Chambers show us that
is no such thing as a divide between the shaping of our inner character and our outward
mission. Better yet, they guide us in practical ways to bridge the two through road-tested
spiritual practices that keep our hearts healthy and our missions vibrant.

TED HARRO, PRESIDENT, RENOVARÉ

Jeremy and Monica are the real deal. They continually give themselves to others for the sake
of the kingdom. In this practical book, they not only share with us concrete spiritual practices
that have helped them draw richly from the river of life, but they also demonstrate how these
practices tangibly help them to live on mission. Drink deeply. Practice regularly. Live freely.

JR WOODWARD, NATIONAL DIRECTOR, THE V3 CHURCH PLANTING MOVEMENT;
AUTHOR, *THE SCANDAL OF LEADERSHIP* AND *CREATING A MISSIONAL CULTURE*

The missional lifestyle must be undergirded by a deep spirituality. In *The Art of Missional
Spirituality*, Jeremy and Monica Chambers have created the perfect guide for developing
these deep roots. Whether revisiting common practices (prayer) or suggesting new ones
(immersion in Ecclesiastes), Jeremy and Monica provide accessible and actionable ideas for
disciples of all levels of experience. I highly recommend this deep and deeply practical tool.

ANGIE WARD, PHD, DIRECTOR, DOCTOR OF MINISTRY PROGRAM AND ASSOCIATE
PROFESSOR OF LEADERSHIP AND MINISTRY, DENVER SEMINARY; AUTHOR, *UNCHARTED
LEADERSHIP: 20 CASE STUDIES TO HELP MINISTRY LEADERS ADAPT TO UNCERTAINTY*

This book is a veritable smorgasbord of ideas, tools, and techniques for how to develop the
kind of Christian spirituality that doesn't draw you away from your neighbors but propels you
into the lives of others and the needs of your city. What a beautiful, rich collection of wisdom,
both ancient and contemporary! You need this book.

MICHAEL FROST, MORLING COLLEGE, SYDNEY

Practical. Inviting. Soul-quenching. Essential! Jeremy and Monica are wise and practiced guides
who know where to find life in the sometimes-scorching landscape of mission. In *The Art of
Missional Spirituality*, they lead us with friendly enthusiasm and genuinely won confidence to
thirty-one gushing springs in the desert. Drink up, friends! You'll be glad you did.

CAROLYN ARENDS, AUTHOR, SINGER, SONGWRITER, AND RENOVARÉ DIRECTOR
OF EDUCATION

An excellent primer for the spiritual disciplines applied to the missionary life. The best part
about this book is the challenge to try and engage in them all … and see what happens.

BRIAN SANDERS, FOUNDER, UNDERGROUND NETWORK; AUTHOR,
UNDERGROUND CHURCH

As a child, God felt like a distant relative who was willing to adopt me, but not really love me, and only as a servant. I didn't know it was possible to have an intimate relationship with a Creator where there is peace, joy, guidance, safety, love, and purpose. This book reinforces the beauty I've discovered in God's love for all of us, connects spiritual rhythms with God's missional heart, and invites us to a path where we can encounter our loving Creator through deep reflection and sacred practices.

AFRIKA AFENI MILLS, FOUNDER AND CEO, CONTINENTAL DRIFT, CHARLOTTE, NC; AUTHOR, *OPEN WINDOWS, OPEN MINDS: DEVELOPING ANTIRACIST, PRO-HUMAN STUDENTS*

The Art of Missional Spirituality is a fundamental guide for Christ-followers actively living on mission for Jesus. Jeremy and Monica have artfully curated thirty-one spiritual practices forged from their own missional living. These are the thirty-one sacred practices that can bring harmony to our busy lives and deeper purpose in our work by helping us fall more deeply in love with Jesus.

BILL COUCHENOUR, DIRECTOR OF DEPLOYMENT, EXPONENTIAL; GOVERNING ELDER, TAMPA UNDERGROUND; COAUTHOR, *UNLEASHED! FINDING EPIC ADVENTURE IN EVERYDAY LIFE*

Jeremy and Monica Chambers capture the simplistic beauty of holistic consecration. By writing from their two distinct personalities, they have crafted a journey that is at once challenging and accessible. Practicing these spiritual disciplines will knit you into deeper intimacy with God and greater connection with your world.

JESSIE CRUICKSHANK, AUTHOR, *ORDINARY DISCIPLESHIP*; FOUNDER, WHOOLOGY; EXECUTIVE MISSIONAL LEADER, THE V3 MOVEMENT

Our culture today can often labor our ministry efforts, bringing on personal exhaustion and weariness. Within these pages, Jeremy and Monica Chambers remind us to slow down and breathe in the goodness of God as we walk the life of a missional practitioner and Jesus-follower.

ROWLAND SMITH, NATIONAL DIRECTOR, FORGE AMERICA; AUTHOR, *LIFE OUT LOUD: JOINING JESUS OUTSIDE THE WALLS OF THE CHURCH*

I have welcomed the reawakening to the importance of spiritual practices in recent years. However, for many, spiritual practices remain tucked away in a box labeled "for spiritual giants" (or those willing to live in a desert). Jeremy and Monica have ripped opened that box with this rich, beautiful, and practical book with a wide range of practices. I cannot wait to share it with people in my church and to recommend it across the networks of which I am a part.

CAM ROXBURGH, SENIOR PASTOR, THE NEIGHBOURHOOD CHURCH, CANADA; INTERNATIONAL DIRECTOR, FORGE MISSIONAL TRAINING; VICE PRESIDENT FOR MISSIONAL INITIATIVES, NORTH AMERICAN BAPTISTS; CONTRIBUTING WRITER ON CHURCH PLANTING AND MISSIONAL THEOLOGY

Jeremy and Monica are luminous, and their joy is contagious. In this book they generously invite us into thirty-one practices that have shaped their vibrant relationship with Jesus and their transformative ministry to others. Come, taste and see that the Lord is good!

MIRIAM (MIMI) DIXON, FORMER SENIOR PASTOR, FIRST PRESBYTERIAN CHURCH, GOLDEN, CO; BOARD OF DIRECTORS, RENOVARÉ; TEACHER, RENOVARÉ INSTITUTE

Dive into *The Art of Missional Spirituality* and experience a powerful thirty-one-day voyage into unparalleled intimacy with Jesus. Through inspired practices and enriching resources, this book stirred my spirit-filled missional life, and it can do the same for you. Don't miss the chance to sit at Jesus' feet and learn from him. This book is a game changer for today's missional practitioners, those who are longing to demonstrate and declare the King and kingdom while nurturing their spiritual growth. Embrace this life-changing journey!

TERRY ISHEE, MISSIONAL PRACTITIONER; EXECUTIVE DIRECTOR, FORGE AMERICA; FOUNDER, NEIGHBORHOOD CHURCH COLLECTIVE, AUSTIN, TX

The Art of Missional Spirituality is aligned with the ethos and thrust of our work with equipping ordinary people in the Kansas City Underground. We train our everyday missionaries in KC to breathe in (tend to your soul) and breathe out (engage in mission in everyday spaces). This is not only echoed but also proclaimed beautifully throughout this book. The thirty-one practices are a vital and valuable resource to help disciples deepen their spirituality while simultaneously unlocking their missional potential.

ROB WEGNER, KANSAS CITY UNDERGROUND; NEWTHING; MICROCHURCH NEXT; COAUTHOR, *THE STARFISH AND THE SPIRIT*

With thirty-one carefully selected spiritual practices, this book is a lifeline for disciples in need of revival. It offers a fresh perspective on connecting intimately with Jesus. If you find your walk with God has gone stale, the practices in this book will breathe new life into your faith. Get ready to experience God's love in new ways and reignite your mission with this invaluable resource.

PETE KELLY, CEO, APARTMENT LIFE; AUTHOR, *31 TRAITS OF CHRIST-CENTERED LEADERS*

In a culture of distraction, reactivity and burn out, Jeremy and Monica remind us of the centrality of missional spirituality—the integration of activity and contemplation as a way of life. This helpful guide plumbs the depths of numerous Christian spiritual practices, equipping us for the road as sent people.

DANIEL SIH, CEO, SPACEMAKERS; MULTI AWARD-WINNING AUTHOR; TEDX SPEAKER

Jeremy and Monica's passion is for every soul to know and love the Trinity with intentionality. The thirty-one practices in this book have biblical precedents, clear explanations with illustrations, abundant key resources, and rhythmic movement toward both known and fresh avenues of missional spirituality.

DR. JAMES AYERS, PROFESSOR EMERITUS, CHURCH AND MINISTRY LEADERSHIP DEPARTMENT, LANCASTER BIBLE COLLEGE/CAPITAL SEMINARY AND GRADUATE SCHOOL

The Art of Missional Spirituality challenges and encourages us that as disciples we can be both fully engaged in the mission of God while also being deeply engaged in communion with God. Jeremy and Monica expertly paint a vibrant picture of the possibility for both, giving the reader a road map with principles and practices to aid our journey toward a lifestyle of deep spiritually and intentional mission.

RICH ROBINSON, COFOUNDER, MOVEMENT LEADERS COLLECTIVE AND CREO

Jeremy and Monica encourage and teach us to close the dangerous gap between intimacy with God and action for God. This book is a practical and rich resource for those seeking to live an authentic life following Jesus, written by a family that is doing it. I'm so thankful for their great example to follow.

STAN DOBBS, FOUNDER AND CEO, LIONHEART CHILDREN'S ACADEMY AND SKYLARK CAMPS; FOUNDER, APARTMENT LIFE, DALLAS, TX

A tremendous blessing! This book weaves a solid biblical foundation that moves readers to powerful spiritual application and practice that helps them passionately pursue Jesus. The mix of scriptural depth and practical exercises will empower any reader to experience a transformative journey with God. The book did a terrific job helping me grow and challenged me to extend the transformation I experienced through the practices into the world around me.

SCOTT MESSNER, PASTOR OF STRATEGIC INITIATIVES, CALVARY CHURCH, LANCASTER, PA

Dallas Willard gave us language to organize Jesus' own practices of spiritual disciplines of abstinence and engagement. His student, Richard Foster, elaborated on these exercises, so that we can not only believe what Jesus taught but also follow him in what he did. Jeremy and Monica Chambers have followed this path with the hope that missional leaders remember that "up toward God" and "in toward community" are joined by "out toward the world." I particularly recommend some innovative chapters, such as "listening to others" and "praying for your enemies." This is wise counsel.

JOHN P. CHANDLER, FOUNDER, WWW.UPTICK.ORG; AUTHOR, *UPTICK: A BLUEPRINT FOR FINDING AND FORMING THE NEXT GENERATION OF PIONEERING KINGDOM LEADERS*

the
art of
missional
spirituality

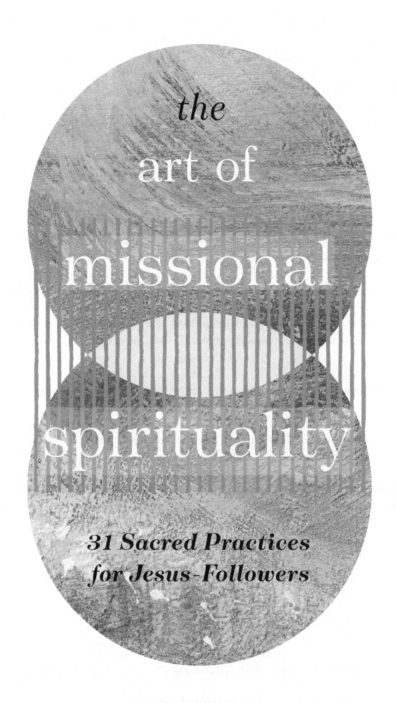

the

art of

missional

spirituality

31 Sacred Practices
for Jesus-Followers

Jeremy Chambers & Monica Paredes Chambers

100 MOVEMENTS
PUBLISHING

First published in 2023 by 100 Movements Publishing

www.100mpublishing.com

Copyright © 2023 by Jeremy Chambers and Monica Paredes Chambers

ISBN 978-1-955142-44-1 (print)

ISBN 978-1-955142-45-8 (e-book)

Cover and interior design: Jude May

Cover images © artbyjulie & Great_Bergens, iStock | jack1e, Adobe Stock

100 Movements Publishing

An imprint of Movement Leaders Collective

Richmond, Virginia

www.movementleaderscollective.com

*Take delight in the L*ORD*, and he will
give you the desires of your heart.*

PSALM 37:4

FORGE
AMERICA

The *Forge America Missional Series* is a collection of books carefully curated for the everyday missional practitioner. As each of us lives on mission for God in the common spaces of life, we often need support and encouragement as we encounter hurdles, doubts, and questions along the way. Written *by* practitioners *for* practitioners, our hope is that each of the titles in this series inspires, equips, and provides invaluable resources for the journey of those who are participating with God on mission.

Forge America is an organization of kingdom-oriented people participating in the mission of God. We are practitioners who cultivate practitioners to follow Jesus in his everyday mission, to be sent in the same way he was sent. We would love to invite you into our community, where we support each other, curate conversation, and engage in training and resources for the missional life.

To find out more about Forge America, please visit www.ForgeAmerica.com and fill out the connection form on our website.

Alternatively, email us at info@forgeamerica.com.

We look forward to meeting you.

> *Again Jesus said, "Peace be with you! As the Father has sent me,*
> *I am sending you."*

JOHN 20:21 NIV

Contents

Foreword

Alan and Debra Hirsch

In this age of hyperactivity, spiritual superficiality, and a desperate scramble for quick fixes, Jeremy and Monica Chambers beckon us into deeper waters. Daringly, they don't offer easy solutions. Instead, they offer something far more potent: spiritual disciplines that anchor the soul, in the same way they have anchored countless missionaries over the centuries in the storms of various missional challenges.

Having walked alongside Jeremy and Monica for years, we've been consistently impressed by their raw authenticity and unyielding commitment to transformative mission work. Their ministry has been a clarion call to many, as they have seeded faith communities in the overlooked areas of our urban landscapes. Their commitment to communicating the all-encompassing love of Jesus is expressed not merely in the words of this book but also in their everyday lives.

To be missional, as many of us have come to realize, requires a dance between contemplation and action. And in this dance, many of us have felt the absence of deep, contemplative rhythms that sustain our action in mission, having been tethered to the shallows of Scripture recitations and transactional prayers. But true prayer, as Jeremy and Monica assert, transcends these shallows. It's an invitation into a profound dialogue with the Divine, one where we are both speakers and listeners, continuously seeking and being sought.

In this book, Jeremy and Monica skillfully bridge the chasm between the practical realities of life and our transcendental wonder of the triune God, crafting a map and guiding readers into deeper realms of God's vision. Recognizing God's intricate imprints, whether in the eyes of a lifelong friend or through a fleeting encounter with a stranger, becomes a mission in itself. It's about discerning those quiet whispers of grace, even amidst the cacophonies of our busy lives.

In the end, this book isn't just a compendium of practices; it's something of a manifesto. Jeremy and Monica challenge us to plunge into the time-tested yet freshly nuanced spiritual disciplines. They ask us to be both ancient and innovative, grounding ourselves in age-old wisdom while also being agile in our contemporary contexts.

In a world buzzing with transient stimuli, this book is a profound call to depth. It reminds us that the infinite lies within, waiting to be discovered. As you traverse this journey with Jeremy and Monica, may you not only encounter the spiritual disciplines they propose but also the pulsating heart of missional life: a life anchored, resonant, and always evolving.

Step into the deeper waters. The adventure awaits.

Both Mission *and* Spirituality

Pastors, church planters, volunteers, and missional practitioners piled into the room, bringing with them a heady mix of vision, commitment, and zeal. But alongside their passion, they also carried the telltale signs of missionary burnout—the hunched shoulders, the drawn faces, the tired eyes of those working hard for the kingdom of God. It was a posture we were all too familiar with.

We, too, had spent many years standing in conference rooms just like that—worshiping, praying, learning, and sharing fervently about the mission God had called us to. And we knew the familiar feeling of burnout: the sense of running on empty, the reality of loneliness, the nagging question in our minds of whether God was really with us as we wholeheartedly pursued what we believed he'd called us to do. We knew all too well how our desire to see fruitfulness in the kingdom had led us to lose sight of the King himself, spiraling into patterns of overwork with little space for knowing the One we were working for and with.

Most of us know the story of Martha in Luke 10, who is encouraged by Jesus to sit at his feet rather than worrying about the work that must be done. When we look at this passage, we often tend to view it as a stand-alone text—one which reminds us to slow down and simply "spend time with Jesus." We forget that the story of Martha is preceded by the parable of the Good Samaritan—a parable that shows us that diligent and sacrificial service for the Lord is a good thing! It sounds great in theory, but how do we balance a life of activism and contemplation without swinging from one extreme to the other? Do we simply need to establish a better work-life balance? Or are there more sustaining and refreshing ways to do the work at hand while constantly drawing life and strength from God?

New Problems, Old Solutions?

Jesus knew how to live out of the overflow of his Father's love; his life demonstrated how intimacy and action can unite. This was evident in both the way he lived and the spiritual practices he engaged in. He feasted *and* fasted. He preached to the crowds *and* sought solitude and silence with his Father. He laid hands on the sick *and* prayed to the One who empowered him to heal. As we'd expect, Jesus perfected the art of missional spirituality.

As followers of Jesus, we're called to imitate his patterns of intimacy and action, and yet throughout the history of the church, many people have struggled to unite the kingdom mission with knowing the King. We tend to separate spiritual intimacy with God from our missional work,[1] compartmentalizing activities as *either* mission (evangelism, good works, ministry service) *or* time with God (worship, prayer, "quiet time"). Mission *for* God and intimacy *with* God are often viewed as separate parts of our lives and potentially as competing "jobs" on our to-do lists. And for those of us actively responding to Jesus' Great Commission, the mission often wins out, as we overlook the importance of growing in knowing the One whom we serve.

Yet following Jesus on his mission is a deeply intimate practice in itself. Jesus, Paul, the early church disciples, and many throughout church history show us that it is possible to be *both* active in the work *and* in union with the Lord. Truly fruitful mission only comes by aligning ourselves with the heart of the One who sends us, engaging in his words, works, and ways because we know who he is, not just what he calls us to. This is what we mean by the term *missional spirituality*. When we spend time more truly knowing God, his eyes of compassion imprint upon us so that we look at the world with his love as we seek to partner with him in his kingdom transformation.

In John 5, Jesus explains to the religious leaders why he can minister in the way he does: "Very truly I tell you, the Son can do nothing by himself; he can do only what he sees his Father doing, because whatever the Father does the Son also does" (verse 19). Just as Jesus was constantly united with his Father, we too must be connected with God. Our ministry cannot be separated from our intimacy with him. The world needs more people who truly look like Jesus, but if we want to look like him, we must commit to knowing HIM who he is.

---

1 By "missional" we are using the historic definition of this term which implies entering into the mission of God. Missional Spirituality, in this sense, is to be truly united with God in his work in this world. It should not, and does not mean professional ministry, guilt-based activity, hyperactivity, achievement focus, or an obsession with productivity, although we recognize that the term "missional" has sometimes been used in these ways within Christian culture.

Practice-Led Learning

Although we often believe that changing our minds will help us to live differently, acting into a new way of thinking is often much more effective. A key understanding in neuroscience is that our brains rewire themselves in response to the external experiences we have and the physical actions we take. This is why our spiritual practices are so important. They expand our minds to know more of God and create new neurological pathways that we take with us into all aspects of our lives. The Lord made the human brain to adapt and change in response to the behaviors we practice, so taking on new practices is an opportunity to not only begin to know God more deeply but to also learn how our relationship with him can be a part of the way we live rather than just how we think.

Spiritual practices have been a way that we (Jeremy and Monica) have discovered the joy of knowing God while on mission with him. Several years ago, after a period of burnout, we found ourselves exploring the spiritual disciplines with renewed interest. As we reengaged with mission and ministry, we discovered that these practices, which helped us to draw near to God, were becoming essential for our survival—we could only operate when we were doing what we saw the Father doing. And the more we practiced these rhythms, the more we uncovered depths of joy and peace not only in our intimacy with God but also with other Christians and those whom God has brought into our lives as we minister. We no longer wanted to do ministry without Jesus beside us. We also discovered that we had so much more love for those around us, almost as if a warmth had returned to us as we experienced the depths of God's love for ourselves and others. It is our prayer that you may also discover this as you practice his presence for these thirty-one days.

We hope these practices will enable you to "taste and see that the LORD is good" (Ps. 34:8). Too many of us believe that time with God is not enjoyable and that there are better ways to spend our time. But this is often because we haven't fully experienced just how good God is. It's similar to our taste buds: if we are accustomed to sugary, processed foods, a natural fruit might not taste as sweet. But if we remove the sugar, our taste buds readjust, and the natural fruit will taste much sweeter. Similarly, when we remove our distractions and make adjustments to the way we use our time and energy, our spiritual "taste buds" can taste the sweetness of being with God.

In these pages, we equip you to engage in practices that Christians have been doing since the time of Jesus. These practices have historically and globally transformed believers to be more like Jesus not only in action but in their very being. After studying and practicing numerous historic, biblical, and modern Christian approaches to developing intimacy with the Lord, we curated a list of thirty-one helpful practices that could be implemented daily for one month and then repeated in an ongoing fashion.[2]

Throughout the book, we've included many of the resources we have found beneficial over the years. We cite a wide range of authors, although it should be noted that just because a work is included, it does not mean we endorse all the author's theological views. Rather, we are aiming to draw from a solid range of historic theological resources, and we exhort the reader to use their discernment when engaging with them.

The practices we share are intended for those who are actively on mission with Jesus, whether in paid ministry or simply throughout their day-to-day lives. We desire that you experience the joy of not only doing things for Jesus but also knowing him intimately as you walk with him in his mission. As pastor and author Skye Jethani says, as we enter into greater intimacy with God, "the line between God's work and ours will disappear."[3] As we become more like Jesus, we testify with our lives to the goodness of his kingdom and its availability right now.

This book is for those who long for more of God's kingdom power in their neighborhoods and communities but are tired of worrying about a lack of resources, wearied by team in-fighting, and frustrated by endless ministry-strategizing that never delivers on its promise. It's for those who are bothered by a form of "discipleship" that doesn't seem to produce lives characterized by love, joy, or peace. It's for those who feel burned-out or close to it. It's for those who long to discover what the Father is doing and how they can partner with him in his mission. It's for those who feel like mission and spirituality pull them in opposite directions.

For all of us who have felt any of those things, maybe it's time for us to return to the Head of the family business, not for a better ministry game-plan, but because if it's not *for* him and *with* him, ~~what~~ are we doing any of this for?

WHY

---

2   These practices were picked from about two hundred options, which we tested and experimented with for a few years, alongside a hundred friends who tried this out and provided feedback. We found the following thirty-one to be the most impactful for us and our friends. These thirty-one practices were first published in a blog: Jeremy Chambers, "31 Days of Delight," *The V3 Movement*, December 24, 2020, http://thev3movement.org/2020/12/24/31-days-of-delight/.

3   Skye Jethani, *What If Jesus Was Serious About Prayer?: A Visual Guide to the Spiritual Practice Most of Us Get Wrong* (Moody, 2021), Scribd ebook, 67.

How to Read This Book

Before you dive into each of the thirty-one practices, below are some pointers on how to get the most out of the practices contained within this book.

- **Think about the posture from which you practice:** Engage in each of these practices prayerfully and in dependence upon the Holy Spirit to minister to your heart. They are a means of turning yourself toward his grace and drawing near to the Lord. They are *not* a means of religious manipulation or superstitious attempts to create self-made spirituality. Make sure you approach each of the practices with the humility of a child asking for help from a good Father. We do these practices because of freedom, because of grace, and because of the goodness God offers freely from his generous hand.[1]

- **Expect one hour of daily commitment:** We know this can be difficult when life is busy, but to allow enough time to read the text and try the practice, we suggest committing one hour each day. Some days may take you less time, but as you may not have experienced some of the practices before, it is helpful to give yourself enough time to digest the information and experience the practice fully.[2]

---

1 Consider the tension of Hebrews 10:14 where it says that he has made us perfect/holy forever through his one act, yet the same passage implies that we are still in the process of being made holy (sanctified). There is an "already/not yet" tension here. We are being sanctified in Jesus because of his work, yet we are called to participate in the sanctification process. Ephesians 2:8–10 also implies this, mentioning that we are saved by grace alone but still called to good works that he has prepared for us. Philippians 2:12–13 also implies this when it calls us to work out our salvation with fear and trembling, yet it affirms that it is God who works in us for our salvation. These tensions are beautiful and biblically sound as they call the attentive student of Jesus to recognize his work within us, while recognizing his call for us to proactively seek to grow in him.

2 If you are pressed for time, we suggest reading the "Purpose" and "Practice" sections and then ignoring the rest of the day's reading and moving on to doing the practice. Of course, in some situations, you may need to read the "Go Deeper" and/or "Savor the Beauty" parts in order to understand the full force and intention of the practice. It is up to you, as the reader and practitioner. You will get out of this what you put into it. Our intention is that each day's reading provides you with a bit more guidance, knowledge for further study, and inspiration for deeper heart-level fellowship and delight in Jesus to try it for yourself.

- **Choose your own adventure:** If you come across a practice and it doesn't feel right, then prayerfully ask, "Why am I resistant to this? Is there anything I can take from this day's reading that would help me grow in intimacy with you, God?" You might choose to adapt a practice slightly. The point is not to stick rigidly to a practice but to allow the practice to launch you into God's presence in whichever way you need.

- **Choose whether to take thirty-one days or fifty-two weeks:** Based on your preferences and season of life, you may want to consider slowing this entire process down and spending a week in each practice. If so, we have included a template for fifty-two weeks for you to explore. (See Appendix 1.)

- **Consider using the additional scriptural study:** Each practice contains references to Scriptures and biblical illustrations. However, if you want to make sure to prioritize the relevant Scriptures then look at the "Key Resources" section for each day, where the first reference provides a Scripture to meditate on. Some of our readers especially enjoy adding this scriptural element directly into their reading and practice.

- **Engage in a maximum of one practice each day:** In order to make this sustainable, we recommend you only practice one thing each day. This will help you to engage more deeply in the practice rather than seeing it as an item to tick off a checklist.

- **Try to embark on this journey with community:** Consider going on this adventure with at least one or two friends. This is fun when done alongside others!

- **Engage in repetition:** Repetition is vital to all learning and allows truths to become ingrained in our lives. We intentionally return to many of the same scriptural points throughout, and we selected key passages that we hope you will desire to linger upon. Repetition of the practices themselves also helps to form positive and life-giving habits of connecting with God.

- **Consider how you can regularly incorporate each practice into your life:** On day thirty-one, there is the opportunity to review which practices you would like to continue, ~~with.~~

Journaling

Purpose

To become attentive to how the Lord is moving in, through, and around you. To become more aware and grateful for God's presence in your life. To learn to reflect and process thoughts, actions, and emotions prayerfully before God.

Go Deeper

There are many different types of journaling, but here we are practicing *prayerful* journaling. Prayerful journaling involves writing (or typing) our thoughts, prayers, and feelings to God in an open and vulnerable way. This can open our eyes to the wonders he is daily orchestrating in and around us. God already knows what our thoughts and feelings are, but he loves for us to come and share openly with him—this is part of how we express our identity as children of God.

Imagine a loved one is in distress. Even though you can clearly see their pain, you still want them to come to you and share openly with you about it because you value their feelings and the relationship. It is the same with God. Because he loves us, he wants us to come to him with how we feel. As we journal, we express what we're experiencing, thinking, and feeling, and we're investing in the intimate relationship he is inviting us into.

Jeremy and I[1] journal very differently from each other. I tend to journal to help me slowly and prayerfully process with God all sorts of emotions and circumstances. If you were to read my journal, you would notice significant intervals between my entries. Whenever I do write, it often looks very much like the psalms of lament. I express my longings for this world to be made whole, detail the difficulties I'm facing in various situations or with certain individuals, and share my wonderings about God's plan when it seems like he is not at work. And I ask God a lot of questions! Journaling serves as a safe space to bring these deep emotions and questions. I know God hears me through what I've written and is attentively listening. This process strengthens my trust in him.

My journal also includes thankful accounts of experiences from God and *memorials of beauty and goodness*. To me, the concept of *memorials of beauty* is similar to the physical symbols created by the Israelites as reminders of God's work (for example, the stone Jacob set up as a pillar in Genesis 28:10–22; or the twelve stones Joshua gave to a representative of each of the twelve tribes in Joshua 4:1–8). When I experience something powerful from the Lord, I often create a tangible reminder I can return to later for the purpose of remembering what he did—it could be a piece of art, writing, or anything else that helps me visualize and recall the magnitude of what he has done.

I (Jeremy) journal in a more analytic way but still use it as a time to slow down, take a deep breath, and draw close to the Lord. I spend time bulleting and outlining my thoughts and observations and collating my thinking into themes and categories. I often write these thoughts as a prayer, and I write poetry or imaginative short stories to express my feelings to God when processing certain life events. I always write expectantly, trusting that the Lord will reply in his way and in his time.

As you approach your journaling, think about how you relate to God. Consider trying out different aspects of journaling that might be a more natural reflection of your way of connecting with him. For example, you may want to journal by pen and paper, or by using a digital document or a text or email thread to yourself. Some people find they prefer to journal by using other artistic mediums of expression, such as mind mapping, doodling, or drawing symbols. You may also be surprised by

---

1   Perhaps we're stating the obvious here, but if we say, "Jeremy and I," you can assume it's Monica speaking, and if we say, "Monica and I," you can assume it's Jeremy.

what you learn when you try methods of journaling that you didn't think were your natural style.

We can see a variety of approaches to the concept of journaling in Scripture: David, Nehemiah, Jeremiah, Luke, Paul, and John were all faith-filled thinkers who took time to listen to the Lord, reflect, interpret, observe, and record their findings.[2] Take note of the diverse writing styles displayed by these authors. Of course, God has breathed and sovereignly chosen his Word to have enduring spiritual authority, but he decided to work through those human authors. If you read the works of David or Solomon in Psalms, Proverbs, and Ecclesiastes, you find they took time to contemplate life and examine their hearts as they explored the joy of relationship with their covenant God. They also explored their pains, struggles, despair, and questions before the Lord. Psalm 88 is an excellent example of the psalmist being extraordinarily honest about their difficulties before the Lord.

Likewise for disciples today, journaling allows us to reflect upon and become attentive to God's glory. This is especially important when we are going through trials and learning to endure difficulty. A little bit of attentiveness to the Lord, especially during seasons of pain and darkness, can enable us to cling to hope in him and to see that he is right there with us. Journaling isn't a one-off experience but instead is part of a journey with God, and so there will be both "mountain-top experiences" and "valley times." The important thing is choosing to connect with God and acknowledge that he is on the journey with us. Journaling is a way of opening our eyes to what he is doing. It takes boldness to pray that daring prayer of Psalm 139, asking the Lord to search us and expose if there is anything in us that we need to surrender to him.

Missional Spirituality

One of the most important things while on mission is to be attentive to what the Lord is doing—in the world around us, in us, through us, and in the people we are connecting with. It can be tempting to stop listening, be inattentive, and just do things out of our own impulses. This can lead to us forgetting to include God in what we're doing. Journaling is a key tool in helping us develop attentiveness, so that we slow down, listen, see what God is doing, watch

---

2   To go deeper, read Nehemiah or any of the biblical authors mentioned above and ask: what sort of relationship did they have with God to be able to write these things? You can also read through Philippians and examine the heart of Paul, or notice David's wide range of experiences throughout the Psalms, or Luke's insights throughout the book of Acts. These were people who understood the value of recording their spiritual experiences, insights, and prayers.

how he is doing it, and, when the time is right, to walk into "the good works that he has prepared for us" (Eph 2:10).[3]

Journaling also enables us to see others—really see them—and love them as Jesus does. In the everyday mission of our lives, we often have a people-group whom we love very much. We want to see these people transformed by hope, love, and goodness. We will need to learn to listen to them rather than pushing our will, pretending to know everything about them, or presuming we have a platform to speak.[4] Journaling helps us to take time to reflect on our surroundings and the people we are serving so that we can surrender and live humbly with those around us. It helps us cultivate a practice of awareness that will lead to more faithful servanthood.

 ## Savor the Beauty

Although many tout the benefits of journaling in terms of "discovering oneself," we must also look at it through the lens of our intimacy with the Father, Son, and Holy Spirit. Although we will discover more about ourselves and how he has beautifully created us, in journaling we also take time to observe the beauty of God, who he is, and how he is at work. If we want to further savor God's beauty, it may help to follow these practices:

- Compile a list of all the remarkable aspects of your relationship with God. (This is what the psalmist did in Psalm 103.)

- Take time to write out the works he has done in your life. (This is what the Gospel writers did.)

- Reflect on God's care for you. (This is what the psalmist did in Psalm 139.)

Don't just write out "attributes of God" as a cold, abstract list, but instead write specific ways you experienced the goodness, beauty, and wonder of the Lord in your life.

You might be reading this and realizing you do not yet find him to be that good or wonderful. Perhaps take time to write out a prayer expressing how you feel and inviting God to show you his glory, just as he revealed himself to Moses on Mount Sinai (Exod. 19) and to the disciples on the Mount of Transfiguration (Matt. 17:5–8).

---

3   In our book *Kingdom Contours*, we discuss "love as real love" and the humility of listening to those we are serving. This practice is a simple way to cultivate humility. Jeremy and Monica Chambers, *Kingdom Contours: Empowering Everyday People With the Tools to Shape Kingdom Movements* (Missional Challenge, 2020), 75–76.

4   Dallas Willard often warned of the dangers of "pushing, presuming, and pretending" when we are looking to share the gospel with others. See Dallas Willard, *Hearing God: Developing a Conversational Relationship with God* (IVP, 2012).

If you ask, seek, and knock, he will respond (Matt. 7:7). This is why James was able to say that the Lord draws near to those who draw near to him (James 4:8). Or perhaps you are in a time of wanting to celebrate God's beauty. Consider simply listing ways you see God's beauty at work in your life and those around you. Whatever season of life we're in, it can be a good practice to regularly journal our thanksgivings—even when life is tough. You could do this annually, monthly, or weekly, and then take the opportunity to reflect on what God was doing in that previous portion of time. Be creative in how you approach this practice.

Practice

Take a reflective inventory of your life with the Lord, and/or write out some prayers in anticipation of the coming month. Here are a few questions to help you get started:

- Why are you going through these thirty-one days?

- What are you longing for the Lord to do in you during this time?

- What might be some of your struggles with committing to this process?

After you have experienced this practice, consider how you might incorporate it as a regular rhythm in your spiritual life. Could you set aside time to journal on a weekly or monthly basis? What style and approach to journaling might help you engage in this practice regularly? Is there a time when it would work well (for example, over breakfast or while waiting in the car) or a particular method that would make it more achievable to continue this practice (for example, using bullet-point journaling or jotting notes on an app on your phone)?

Key Resources

- Study the book of Nehemiah to see his example of journaling.

- ✓2 Corinthians 13:5.

- Adele Ahlberg Calhoun, *Spiritual Disciplines Handbook: Practices that Transform Us* (IVP, 2015). See section on journaling.

- Donald Whitney, *Spiritual Disciplines for the Christian Life* (NavPress, 2014). See section on journaling.

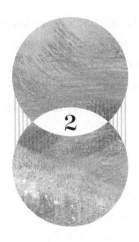

Fasting and the
Welcome Prayer

Purpose

To learn we don't need to let food or material things control us and that we can feast on God and experience his sustenance. To learn to receive from God anything he brings to our day by welcoming him in prayer and trusting him with our lives.

Go Deeper

To follow Jesus is to imitate him. Jesus began his entire ministry with a forty-day fast (Matt. 4:2; Luke 4:2). So when we undertake a small fast for one meal or one day, we take a small step toward identifying with Christ. As we contemplate our hunger pains, we can consider that Jesus experienced the same but at a much greater level.

Fasting is a way of discovering our sole dependence on God and learning the truth that we do not live by bread alone but by every word that proceeds from the mouth of God (Deut. 8:3; Matt. 4:4). The Lord has made our bodies. He is the One who holds them together. When we choose to practice something that involves our bodies, we show both ourselves and God that we are committed to him. Fasting allows us to feast on God and experience his fully satisfying nourishment. As we do this, we begin to feel a loosening in our dependence on material things, recognizing we don't need to depend on something physical to fill those deep parts of our being. As Jesus told us in Matthew 6, we don't have to worry about what we will eat, what we will wear, or how we will be provided for because we are exceedingly valuable to God, and he will always take care of us.

Fasting is also a means of training ourselves to say no to urges, building self-discipline and resolve. Fasting places us before God in our true state of weakness. It is humbling to realize just how fickle we are; how easily our emotions can move from positive to negative, just because we're hungry. These challenges and frustrations provide ideal opportunities to say no, redirect our focus, and find satisfaction in God as we turn instead to him. Many Christians today seem to resist fasting from food, choosing instead to fast from something else. But the fasts in Scripture tend to be fasts from food. Try to release to the Lord your desire for comfort through eating and allow him to sustain you with his spiritual nourishment.[1] We don't do these practices to earn God's favor or to achieve self-righteousness, but instead out of a desire to cultivate more awareness of God's goodness, his lordship in our lives, and the freedom and grace he offers us.

In conjunction with the practice of fasting, it is worth considering a welcome prayer to invite Jesus' intentions into your day. This prayer can stir up gratitude in us, as we recognize God at work in the blessings throughout the day, as well as in the difficulties. Having regularly experimented with fasting individually and communally over the years, Monica and I have noticed the tendency for those fasting to take it lightly or just "skip a meal" without replacing that meal with intentional intimacy with Jesus. So by bringing a welcome prayer into our day, we posture ourselves from the outset to be ready to receive from the Lord while fasting, ready to turn our hunger into a reminder to focus on Christ.[2]

A welcome prayer can be as simple as saying, "Welcome" to challenging events or circumstances. Through this prayer, we acknowledge God is lovingly in control and has a wise plan.

We like to use this prayer from spiritual coach and author Jerome Daley:

---

1 Be discerning of any health or psychological issues that would make this practice problematic for you.
2 If the welcome prayer intrigues you, then check out Richard Foster's book, *Prayer: Finding the Heart's True Home* (HarperOne, 2002) and read his chapter on "The Prayer of Relinquishment," which gives helpful teaching on a prayerful pattern of yielding to the Lord in all circumstances.

Welcome, Holy Spirit. I welcome everything that [happens] to me today because I know it's for my good. [...] I let go of my agenda for affection and approval by receiving my belovedness. Welcome, Holy Spirit. I let go of my agenda for safety and security by resting in your abundance. Welcome, Holy Spirit. I let go of my agenda for power and control by surrendering to your grip on my life. Welcome, Holy Spirit. I let go of my desire to change anyone or anything or even myself. I open myself to your presence and action within me today.[3]

Choosing to "feast" on God can feel like a difficult concept to understand. But in practice, this is about choosing to put our attention back on him, even when our physical desire is to think about food (or our lack of food!). Feasting can be as simple as worshiping, reading the Bible, and praying. You might choose to draw on some of the other spiritual practices in this book as a way to focus your attention on God.

Jeremy and I have occasionally facilitated a "24 hours of prayer" event, where people in our community sign up for one-hour slots to come and pray. One time, we hosted such an event in our apartment and aimed to fast for the majority of the time, with only some sleep and a little bit to eat throughout the day. But, surprisingly, neither Jeremy nor I experienced any hunger during this whole time. Miraculously, we felt our whole beings fully nourished, and there was no fatigue as we prayed with the community. It was as if we were feasting so deeply on God that our need to eat food was unnecessary.[4] This is what it means to feast on God![5]

Fasting can have varying degrees of difficulty in different seasons, so it is vital to pay attention to what is best for you right now. If fasting is not a life-giving practice for you currently, acknowledge this and see if there is some way the Lord may be calling you to respond. The key principle is that we are *reducing something (of material value)* in order to allow *something else (of spiritual value) to increase* in our lives.

---

3 Jerome Daley, *Gravitas: The Monastic Rhythms of Healthy Leadership* (NavPress, 2020), 110.
4 We do not recommend abstaining from sleep, nor extreme fasting, but we share this story as an example that the Lord can do some unique activity when you decide to place him first.
5 You can read more about this experience in a blog post we wrote: https://thev3movement.org/2018/06/11/24-hour-prayer-fuel-movement/.

Missional Spirituality

Jesus fasted before beginning his ministry (Matt. 4:1–11). We too can incorporate fasting as a regular practice to help deepen our intimacy with God and propel us to follow Jesus into his mission in the lives of those around us. Fasting can give us clarity on the things that are important and also trains us to stay vigilant and sober-minded. After fasting, Jesus was able to resist the temptations of the devil, drawing from the strength of Scripture. Similarly, the disciples and the early church often fasted before making important decisions.[6]

The welcome prayer is an essential practice as we engage in everyday mission. It allows us to ask, "How can I have a loving response to God, others, and myself in this moment?" Every day, things come our way that are unexpected and sometimes seemingly undesirable. However, if we yield to the Lord, remember the promise that "in all things, God works for the good of those who love him" (Rom. 8:28), and pray accordingly, then our attitude toward God, self, and others will be set right. Instead of trying to control situations or events, we can invite God to intervene and show us what our posture should be. Moments of frustration can be transformed into moments of grateful surrender.

Savor the Beauty

Notice how fasting causes you to detach temporarily from something you were relying on. In place of what you are fasting from, you will need to find something else to sustain you. It's all too easy to enter a fast only to distract yourself from the difficulties of fasting; don't make this mistake. The idea of feasting on the Lord means we can experience the deep joy that comes when we receive sustenance directly from him. Initially, fasting may seem challenging, but as you gradually embrace this practice in a non-legalistic manner, you will discover it is deeply restful.

Returning to a welcome prayer throughout the day serves as a reminder to seek the goodness and beauty of the Lord. When the unexpected comes our way, when we feel weary, "hangry," or unable to rely on our own strength and resources, the welcome prayer helps us focus back on God. We can ask him to give us his power to persevere and respond well to whatever we are facing. We invite the joy of the Lord to

---

6   See Acts 9:9, 13:2–3, 14:23, 27:9.

be our strength (Neh. 8:10), and as we navigate through our difficulties, we discover that as we commit time to seek God a hidden opportunity is revealed; our misery is transformed into gentle intimacy with him.

Practice

Fast for at least one meal or the whole day. Open your time of fasting by saying a welcome prayer. In place of the time you would have spent eating, focus on the Lord in whatever ways help you to connect with him. Throughout the day, be intentional about allowing those moments of hunger or "earthly lack" to drive you into his presence. Learn to pay attention to the lack in order to find his abundance. When you feel hungry, tired, or annoyed at the experience, use the opportunity to turn your attention to God as the One who can fulfill your deepest needs. You could try repeating a welcome prayer at those times or having set times when you say a welcome prayer again.

After you have experienced this practice, consider how you might incorporate it as a regular rhythm in your spiritual life. Could you fast on a weekly or monthly basis? Are there times when you have decisions to make when it would be appropriate to fast as part of listening to God?

Consider how this practice might become part of your rhythm in a meaningful way. Fasting may not be beneficial when you're busy, as the distractions of work and life could limit you from time with God. When you do fast, how could you carve out time to say the welcome prayer throughout your day (for example, pausing before you drive somewhere, taking a walk instead of a lunch break, or using moments like washing your hands to pray)?

As you experience some of the other spiritual practices in this book, are there any that complement fasting as a way for you to feast on God during these times? How might you engage in this practice with your community, encouraging one another to persevere and experience God's joy together?

Key Resources

- Isaiah 58:6–7.

- Matthew 6:16–18.

- John Mark Comer, "Fasting: Practicing the Way," https://practicingthewayarchives. org/practices/fasting. This article makes note of the purposes of fasting in starving the flesh/feeding the spirit, fasting as prayer, and fasting for solidarity with the poor.

- Jerome Daley, *Gravitas: The Monastic Rhythms of Healthy Leadership* (NavPress, 2020).

- Richard Foster, *Celebration of Discipline: The Path to Spiritual Growth* (Harper, 2002), chapter four.

- Richard Foster, *Prayer: Finding the Heart's True Home* (HarperOne, 2002). See chapter on "Prayer of Relinquishment."

- Jan Johnson, *Simplicity and Fasting: Spiritual Disciplines Bible Studies* (IVP Connect, 2013).

- John Piper, *A Hunger for God: Desiring God through Fasting and Prayer* (Crossway, 2013).

Solitude and Silence

Purpose

To bring stillness and quiet into our day in order to experience a deeper intimacy with God and awareness of his presence.

Go Deeper

In his book *Devotional Classics*, theologian and author Richard Foster says:

Solitude is one of the deepest disciplines of the spiritual life because it crucifies our need for importance and prominence. Everyone— including ourselves at first—will see our solitude as a waste of good time. We are removed from "where the action is." That, of course, is exactly what we need. In silence and solitude God slowly but surely frees us from our egomania. In time we come to see that the really important action occurs in solitude. Once we have experienced God at work in the soul, all the blare and attention of the world seem like a distant and fragmentary echo. Only then are we able to enter the hustle and bustle of today's machine civilization with perspective and freedom.[1]

Perhaps there is nothing more deeply restful for the soul than silence and solitude, but this requires significant intentionality. In our overstimulated world, silence and solitude are something we rarely experience. To pursue this practice, we will have to make time and find space to get away from the chaos of modern life.

The prize of this practice is the ability to enjoy God's presence without distraction, slowing down and remembering his goodness. How beautiful this can be! God is waiting for you, constantly longing for you to draw near to him. His presence is always accessible, but the busyness of our lives means we so often forget it's available. This practice allows you to take a step deeper into a conscious and intentional connection with the Lord.

Often people avoid this practice because they feel they can't do it "perfectly," but this is about showing up and being willing to see what happens in your time with God. There are many times when I (Monica) will finish ten or fifteen minutes of silence and feel like my mind was all over the place. But the fact that I showed up and *practiced* focusing my mind back on the Lord is exactly what needed to happen. As our friend and Richmond missional leader, Don Coleman, once said, "The very fact that someone sat down to be with the Lord is already a miracle; it is victory enough." The point is not to achieve but rather to be transformed. Over the years, I have had to wrestle with feeling I needed to be productive during my time of silence. However, one time I sensed God saying, "Monica, would you be willing to waste time on me? Can you love me in this way? Can you believe that I am in control and have all the abundance of time so you can spend fifteen minutes resting and delighting in my presence, just for my own sake?" These questions struck my heart and helped me to release my compulsion to produce something and, instead, moved me toward resting in God's presence.

It's important to bear in mind that during our practice we won't always experience something epic. This is a practice of faith, in which we draw near to the Lord and turn from the tyranny of the urgent, even when we may not feel God's presence. Regardless of how we feel, we believe he is actively there with us in the silence. Sometimes he might say something; sometimes he might not. I like to think of this practice as akin to being in the company of someone we deeply love, where we can simply sit on the

---

1   Richard Foster, *Devotional Classics: Selected Readings for Individuals and Groups* (HarperCollins, 2005), 85.

couch in a silent embrace. God wants to enjoy the silence with us as well, and this quiet time with God can be as intimate an experience as when he speaks to us clearly through his Word or his Spirit.

We will have some days when we more easily enter silence and solitude before God and others when it's harder. That's ok. Just come before the Lord in your weakness, with all your fleeting thoughts and to-do lists, and allow being with him to bring you peace and stillness, drawing near to you as you draw near to him.

Missional Spirituality

For those of us who regularly engage in the mission of God in this world, we are most prone to forgetting to slow down. Burnout, depression, and addictions, as well as weariness at the uncontrollable pace of life, are common in ministry leaders and volunteers. Jeremy and I have both been through a season of burnout, which took a few years to recover from. During that time, we had a keen sense that Jesus was carrying us with his precious love, as he restored our souls. The practice of silence and solitude was instrumental in bringing healing to our bodies, minds, and souls. The Lord allowed us to discover him afresh within the quietness. We even moved into a new apartment afterward and named it "The Stillness," because we would spend time each day sitting or silently walking and praying. After experiencing burnout, prayer became a much more essential element in our ministry and mission, and, unsurprisingly, we noticed the Lord started doing some amazing things that required less typical "human work" from us.

As we all engage with our world, we are exposed to some dark realities of life. We often come directly into contact with brokenness, and we can face intense spiritual warfare. The practice of silence and solitude is a way to pause from the busyness and consume the grace Jesus is offering us. It serves as a way to gain clarity of mind and heart, allowing us to process the things that may have been distracting us. It is a distraction-removal practice that can be deeply impactful in every area of our lives.

Jeremy and I have also seen how engaging in silence and solitude can affect how we listen to those around us. As we become more comfortable with silence, we no longer feel we have to come up with something to say or find the words that will "fix" a situation. Instead, we can give someone the gift of being listened to. When people have been listened to well, they open up about things they wouldn't have otherwise shared. We have also seen the effects of this practice on our bodies. Sometimes when we are with others, we take a moment for a deep breath and draw upon the experience we have gained through longer times of silence. (This can also involve changing our posture physically.) After taking this moment, we are often calmer, more at peace, and better able to demonstrate the good news of Jesus in the way we relate to others—sometimes even simply through our relaxed posture.

Savor the Beauty

Perhaps it is in silence and solitude that we find the ability to see God more clearly than in many other places in life. God's presence, goodness, and truth become more evident. When we stop running around and slow down, quieting the noise around us, and even our inner voice, we discover God has been there all along, caring for us and speaking to us. As we practice this more and more, our experience of silence and solitude can shift from frustration or difficulty to enjoyment. When Jeremy and I first started this practice, we couldn't wait for the minutes to go by and the timer to go off. However, now we feel enjoyment at the wonderful and restful time, sometimes wishing for longer or even extending our time.

Practice

Decide upon a time in your day when you can be alone and silent before the Lord. This doesn't mean you fill the time with reading, prayer, or listening to worship music, but rather you stop and allow complete silence. Psalm 46:10 says, "Be still and know that I am God." Perhaps start your time by reading Psalm 131, and then sit for a while and ask the Lord to reveal himself to you in a fresh way. This practice can be as simple as stepping aside from your busyness and finding a quiet, empty place to sit and be silent before the Lord.

Jeremy tends to enjoy silence and solitude in desolate places, like a closet, a library, or an empty parking lot. (He loves places with minimal stimulus.) On the other hand, I love to do this near water and trees or plants to allow God's creation to remind me of his love and creativity. Experiment with different settings to find what's best for you.

If you find it difficult to practice this, begin by giving yourself ten minutes. Once you have regularly practiced this shorter time, God will expand your capacity to sit and enjoy his presence for longer.

If you have young children at home, this may feel like an impossible practice! However, many of our friends with kids have commented that although it can be challenging to engage in silence and solitude with their little ones around, they have discovered creative solutions. For some, this may mean taking time while the baby is napping, or when they are waiting in the car to pick up their kids from an event. Some even combine their silent time by helping their children enjoy a quiet time for themselves as well. Parents who have managed to embrace this practice have rightly said that we will always find a way to do what we value most. If we value the presence of God, we will find ways to connect with him even in the rhythms of a full life. It requires choosing to not let the busyness of life push him out.

After you have experienced this practice, consider how you might incorporate it as a regular rhythm in your spiritual life. Even ten minutes of regular silence and solitude will make a difference, and perhaps you could look to do longer times on a monthly or yearly basis.

Key Resources

- Psalm 46:10.

- Lamentations 3:28.

- Habakkuk 2:20.

- Mark 1:35.

- Luke 5:16.

- Shelley Trebesch, *Isolation: A Place of Transformation in the Life of a Leader* (VistaGroup Consulting, 1997).

- Dallas Willard, *The Divine Conspiracy: Rediscovering Our Hidden Life in God* (Harper, 1998). Chapter nine is one of the most excellent treatments of this subject.

Praying Psalm 23 and the Lord's Prayer

Purpose

To take a few moments in our day to return to who God is and how he leads us. To remember his shepherding heart for us. To allow these biblical passages to become truth for us and transform every area of our lives.

Go Deeper

Monica and I love this practice! Years ago, someone challenged me to read, recite, or pray through Psalm 23 and the Lord's Prayer (Luke 11) each day. So I accepted the challenge and ended up never stopping. Over the past few years, hardly a day has gone by when I haven't connected with these passages in some way; they have changed our lives.[1] We find ourselves frequently sharing these Scriptures with others or praying them when we are going through difficulties. Whenever we feel we are in the "valley of the shadow of death," we are reminded we

---

1 You can hear more about our personal story with this practice on the *Renovaré Podcast*. "Monica and Jeremy Chambers—Getting Personal with the Lord's Prayer," produced by Nathan Foster, *Renovaré Podcast*, April 14, 2023, https://renovare.org/podcast/monica-and-jeremy-chambers-getting-personal-with-the-lords-prayer.

do not need to fear evil, that we can request the Lord deliver us, and recognize that the Good Shepherd is always with us. Psalm 23 is a psalm of abundance—the abundance that comes from God being our Shepherd, and we therefore lack nothing. Out of this truth comes all the rest of the psalm.

In recent years, the Lord's Prayer has particularly impacted me (Monica). This prayer holds special significance as it was the prayer Jesus gave his disciples—who had been observing Jesus' prayer life for some time—when they sought his guidance on how to pray. I have used this prayer to lead me in my prayers, as a framework for my requests. And it also serves to remind me of who God is.

Both Psalm 23 and the Lord's Prayer are so rich and full of the reality of God and his kingdom. They speak of God as our Father, the Holy One, the One who is enacting his goodness in the world around us, our Provider, the One who forgives, and the One who is ultimately Ruler over all. It's easy to assume that our experiences of this world are the way life is, but in God's kingdom we can live with no lack and can trust in our Good Shepherd to lead us in his ways.

Jeremy and I have found there is something especially powerful about revisiting a passage three times throughout the day. In the morning these passages give vision and purpose. They remind us of the courage, faith, and resilience we can have, no matter what happens. To return to them at noon makes our midday meal more sacred as we eat with gratitude, looking back at how God has already been with us in the morning. It also enables us to think ahead to the rest of the day with intentionality and attentiveness to what Jesus is doing around us. To return to these passages in the evening is a sweet way to close the day with a reminder of his goodness and faithfulness. It also helps us sleep better as our minds are filled with his fullness just before we lie down.

Missional Spirituality

In our everyday mission, many of us easily forget that the Lord is our Shepherd, and he is the Shepherd of those we are ministering with or ministering to. We're also quick to forget that we are partnering with him to see *his* kingdom come and *his* will being done, not *our* kingdom or will being done. By incorporating these passages into the rhythm of our day, week, or month we are reminded that God is God, and we are his servants. We need the experiences Psalm 23 describes—lying down in green pastures, having our souls restored—but if we are in the habit of following our own lead instead of God's, it is all too easy for us to forget to slow down and rest in him.

In the Lord's Prayer, we are reminded that he is *our* Father. This spiritual journey isn't simply individualistic but instead, *we* as the people of God have a common Father. We are siblings in Christ. Too often, especially in ministry circles, we become territorial and forget we are partnering with our siblings in Christ for his kingdom work. Praying these passages in response to the anxieties and fears that arise from various ministry difficulties can remind us that we are one family, pursuing a greater mission together.

Savor the Beauty

Psalm 23 and the Lord's Prayer are a template for how we can be led by God throughout the entirety of our lives. In praying these passages, we invite the shepherding guidance of the Lord into any situation we face. There is a sense of journey to both of these Scriptures. As I (Jeremy) have been praying both almost daily for five years, I have found that the more I spend time in these verses, the more curious I am to explore them even further. These passages continue to open up entirely new dimensions of faith and insight into my life, as if I am discovering them for the first time. I find they are even more powerful as I go through all sorts of circumstances, from the greenest pastures to the darkest valleys. I even notice these passages manifesting in my prayer life and in the way I talk with others. Within these passages we can find connection and comfort as we pray through them in any situation or eventuality we may be facing. Any aspect of God's character we need to draw upon is evident in these verses.

Practice

Meditate on Psalm 23 and the Lord's Prayer in the morning, at noon, and in the evening. Read through either (or both) of these passages, allowing the words to connect deeply with you as you reflect on the reality of who God is. (You are welcome to use another passage if you prefer. We have chosen these Scriptures because of the powerful recurring themes contained within them.)

As you meditate on the passages, consider how the truths contained within these verses affect all areas of your life. You could recite the verses out loud, write them down, or sing them through a worship song. Whatever you do, aim to return to these passages three times throughout your day.

After you have experienced this practice, consider how you could use some of the creative ways mentioned above to engage with the passages. Perhaps you could read them in the morning, sing or listen to them in song form at midday, and pray them out loud in the evening.

Some of our friends have found meditating on these passages to be helpful when their sleep is disrupted at night. Are there times and places where you feel discouraged, and a practice of reciting Scripture could bring peace and encouragement?

Key Resources

- Thomas Watson, *The Lord's Prayer* (Banner of Truth, 1960).

- Dallas Willard, *Life Without Lack: Living in the Fullness of Psalm 23* (Nelson Books, 2019).

- Many authors have written on the Lord's Prayer, including N. T. Wright, Elmer Towns, Rick Warren, Al Mohler, R. C. Sproul, Pope Francis, Warren W. Wiersbe, John Ortberg, and Tim Chester.

Contemplative Prayer

Purpose

To contemplate God's presence, savoring our relationship with him and trusting that as we draw near to him, he will receive us with open, restful arms.

Go Deeper

Contemplative prayer is simply a means of allowing the reality of God to be impressed upon us.[1] In the *Spiritual Disciplines Handbook*, Adele Calhoun describes contemplative prayer this way:

Just as friends can enjoy one another without conversing, contemplative prayer is a way of being with God without wordiness. In contemplative prayer we rest and wait. Keeping our hearts alert and awake to the presence of God and his Word, we listen. Psalm 131 contains a wonderful image of a weaned child stilled and quieted in

---

1 This is not to be confused with New Age concepts of "contemplation," which many readers may be concerned with; here we are simply offering a posture of prayerful meditation (as Psalm 1 speaks of) with respect to the Lord.

its mother's arms. A weaned child isn't looking to nurse. A weaned child comes to the mother for love and communion. The psalmist writes: "I have stilled and quieted my soul; like a weaned child with its mother, like a weaned child is my soul within me."[2]

In the busyness of our lives, we can easily forget God's presence. But God is as present as a mother cradling her child. Babies take several months to develop something called "object permanence." This is where they know that something exists, even when they can no longer see it. Before this has developed, they literally forget their parents, toys, and anything else as soon as it is not in view. In our spiritual lives, we can be a bit like babies who haven't yet learned object permanence. As soon as something else draws our focus, it's as if God doesn't exist; we forget about his presence.

Jesus encouraged the disciples with the promise that he would send his Spirit so they would be filled permanently with his presence (John 15:26), and at Pentecost this became a reality for all who choose to follow him—both then and now (Acts 2). We also recognize that God is omnipresent; he fills the heavens and the earth (Jer. 23:24). If we believe this, we should look for God's presence around us, becoming more aware of him. If he dwells within us, why wouldn't we pause to perceive him from time to time?

Throughout church history, many have described contemplative prayer as a movement from *thoughts* of God toward *being* with God.[3] Centering prayer and breath prayer (see pages 135–139) are historical examples of how the early Christians embraced contemplative prayer. They would take a word or phrase from Scripture, pray it before the Lord, and allow it to be a truth that would ground them and help them to abide in him. This isn't the vain repetition Jesus warned about (Matt. 6:7), but rather a way to turn our thoughts toward the Lord and the things above (Col. 3:2). After repeatedly reciting this prayer over a period of time, the ancient Christians would find themselves slowing down and gaining a profound sense of being in the

---

2   Adele Calhoun, *Spiritual Disciplines Handbook: Practices that Transform Us* (IVP, 2015), 240.

3   Some authors who testify to this contemplative connection with the Lord include John Calvin, Jonathan Edwards, Teresa of Avila, François Fénelon, Jeanne Guyon, Brother Lawrence, Frank Laubach, Martin Luther, Augustine, and the more recent Richard Foster—but this is only a fraction of those who experience this. Although some of those authors are noted as "mystics," we must read them in context, paying attention to what is actually being said and taking note of their Christ-obsessed focus. Over the years, incorrect assumptions have been made about some of these authors, causing many in the church to reach certain conclusions without ever having diligently studied their works.

presence of the Lord without needing to speak any words. Practicing contemplative prayer is about resting in his love for us and our love for him. It may begin with meditating on Scripture or a characteristic of God or noticing his handiwork in the world. As we contemplate these things, we become aware of God's presence in and around us.

Missional Spirituality

There are many names for the Holy Spirit, including Advocate, Helper, Comforter, and Counselor. In sending us his Spirit, Jesus ensured we would have the presence and the power of the triune God with us to help us in our missional work—to rejuvenate, guide, and comfort us. Contemplative prayer while on mission is magnificently good for the soul. For those stepping into spiritual and missional leadership, knowing God's presence is vital. It isn't about *what we do* in ministry as much as *who we are* in Jesus and *how we allow Jesus to overflow through us*. Our lives will demonstrate the effects of being in an intimate relationship with the Trinity.

Throughout the apostle Paul's life, there were significant periods he spent with the Lord. We don't know all the details, but even before he was commissioned and sent out from Antioch, he spent some time out in the desert seeking the Lord (Gal. 1:13–18).[4] Consider the foundation this gave him as a missionary. He learned to be with God in the wilderness, where he couldn't rely on activity to feel good about himself or on others to affirm him. He discovered how to live by dependence on the Lord alone. Growing in this awareness of God's presence was what sustained him when he was in the throes of missional work, facing trials and persecution. Likely, this experience enabled him to make such bold declarations as, "I consider everything a loss because of the surpassing worth of knowing Christ Jesus my Lord, for whose sake I have lost all things" (Phil. 3:8).

Savor the Beauty

I (Jeremy) have always known God is beautiful and good, but it wasn't until I learned to quiet myself, rest before him, and really pay attention

---

4 Charles Stanley, "What Happened to Paul in the Desert?" *Christianity.com*, November 28, 2011, https://www.christianity.com/jesus/early-church-history/the-apostle-paul/what-happened-to-paul-in-the-desert.html.

to his presence that I began to understand the depth of his beauty and goodness. I increasingly discovered that he grants incredible joy, peace, and love to those who simply spend time recognizing and being in his presence. As we practice contemplative prayer, we open our eyes and see and dwell on God's many facets, just like when we look into the eyes of someone we love as we hold and cherish them.

Practice

Take around ten to fifteen minutes in a quiet and distraction-free space. Start by asking God to reveal himself to you and that you would recognize his presence. You might want to focus on a particular Bible verse or on a repeated line of prayer such as "Come, Lord Jesus." Or you might choose to meditate on a particular aspect of God's character. When Jesus left his disciples he said, "Behold, I am with you always, even until the end of the age" (Matt. 28:20 ESV). Contemplate this truth and consider how much you really know and believe this.

As you continue with your time, move beyond merely thinking about him to *being with him and in him.* Reflecting on John 15 and Psalm 84 is excellent for this practice. Try to direct your full attention to recognizing the reality of God's presence with you.

After you have experienced this practice, consider how you could practice being aware of God's presence in natural "quiet" moments during your day—as you wake up, over a coffee, or when you are out in nature. Perhaps try to do this practice outside of your usual time with God, so you aren't distracted by your usual ways of relating to God that are more thought-based (such as reading long Bible passages and intercessory prayer). These practices can be done as well, but they will divert your attention away from being simply aware of God's presence.

Key Resources

- 2 Corinthians 3:17–18; and 4:18.

- Ken Boa, *Conformed to His Image: Biblical, Practical Approaches to Spiritual Formation* (Zondervan Academic, 2020). All his chapters about prayer are useful reading.

- François Fénelon, *Christian Perfection* (Harper & Row, 1947) and *Maxims of the Mystics* (Mowbray, 1909).

- Richard Foster, *Prayer: Finding the Heart's True Home* (HarperOne, 2002). See chapter on contemplative prayer.

- Richard Foster, *Sanctuary of the Soul: A Journey into Meditative Prayer* (Hodder & Stoughton, 2012). This is a most excellent and easy-to-read resource on contemplative prayer.

- Brother Lawrence and Frank Laubach, *Practicing His Presence* (Christian Books Pub House, 1973).

- Brother Lawrence, *The Practice of the Presence of God: Being Conversations and Letters of Nicholas Herman of Lorraine (Brother Lawrence)* (Martino Fine Books, 2016).

- Saint Teresa of Avila, *The Interior Castle* (Tan Books, 2011).

Studying Scripture

Purpose

To discover the benefits of understanding Scripture as it illuminates our knowledge of who God is and the nature of his relationship with us. To lose any hindrances or obstacles we face when studying the Bible and discover afresh that God is revealing himself intimately through his Word.

Go Deeper

Jeremy and I considered calling this practice "a sacrificial investment into study" because the aim is to spend significant time delving into Scripture. In Hosea 4:6 the Lord says, "My people are destroyed from lack of knowledge." This is sadly true for many Christians today and may account for some of the challenges the church experiences. It can seem like people are following the world more than they are following God. Although occasional, personal Bible reading may be increasing,[1] it is rare to find those who regularly and confidently

---

1 In a recent survey, Barna found an increase in those whom they define as "Bible Users," meaning they "read, listen to, or pray with the Bible on their own at least three or four times a year outside of a church service or church event." See "State of the Bible 2021: Five Key Findings," *Barna*, May 19, 2021, https://www.barna.com/research/sotb-2021/.

study the Word. What a difference it could make if we significantly invested ourselves in reading God's Word of life!

To study the Bible is to approach the Scriptures as a student of the text but also as an apprentice of Jesus himself. There are numerous different methods of Bible study, all of which can help illuminate God's Word to us. (See the Key Resources section at the end of this chapter for some tools.) This practice requires us to come with humility, slowing down, and prayerfully asking the Spirit to reveal what we need. We ask the Lord to meet us, transform us, and open our eyes, building our faith and imprinting his way of thinking upon us, thereby truly renewing our minds. We allow space for curiosity, analysis, meditation, and encounter, having faith that the Lord will meet us and instruct our hearts and minds. In Romans 12:2, Paul tells the church to "be transformed by the renewal of your mind" (ESV). If our minds are in constant need of renewal, we need God's Word to help us accomplish this.

Psalm 1 tells us there is a blessing for the person who meditates on the Word of God "day and night" (verse 2). This means that meditation, serious consideration, and seeking an understanding of God's Word are good and profitable. So when studying Scripture feels challenging, we know God will bless us through it. It may feel like a sacrifice in our schedule or that it's not our natural way of connecting with the Lord, but he asks us to love him with all that we have: heart, *mind*, soul, and strength (Mark 12:30). He has given us our minds so that we might know him and his goodness more deeply. When we apply our minds to studying his Word, we allow God's thoughts and views of the world to fill us.

Some people perceive studying and applying our minds toward God as a less spiritual experience. However, when our minds are opened up by the Holy Spirit, we discover more of who God is and who we are, and it gives us the opportunity to live differently. For some of us, studying may feel too rigid or constraining. However, if we come with a humble heart, longing to experience revelation, God—the perfect teacher—always reveals more to us than we expect, enriching and comforting us in the process.

Missional Spirituality

There have been seasons when Jeremy and I have struggled with the typical Bible study approach to Christianity. Perhaps we have seen those we've judged to be "Bible people"—full of biblical data but seemingly lacking in love—and we've failed to see the benefits of study. Perhaps this is one of the reasons so many Christians have given up on the practice of Bible study. As missionally-minded people, it's easy to feel somewhat self-righteous about this as we see ourselves as doers of the Word, not simply hearers. Both of us have repeatedly had to turn away from that heart of self-righteousness!

The best biblical scholars of Jesus' day were the Pharisees, and Jesus warned people not to be like them for they were hypocrites (Matt. 23). However, Jesus also prayed in John 17:17 that the Father would sanctify his disciples "by the truth," and that his Word is the truth. Think about this for a moment: Jesus asked the Father to use the power of truth. This implies that the mere presence of Scripture doesn't automatically sanctify unless the Father orchestrates it to do so. In the same way, if we are to be transformed by the Word, we need to read it with the plea that the Spirit of God will sanctify our hearts and draw us into the beauty of his holiness.

As we study the Word of God, we also experience it as a commissioning and enabling catalyst for mission. This practice is about allowing our minds to be aligned with his mind, his thoughts influencing our thoughts, and the God of mission imbuing our hearts with his heart. Many notable missionaries throughout history have found biblical study to be a critical source of ongoing sustenance, including William Carey, Adoniram and Ann Judson, David Livingstone, Hudson Taylor, Amy Carmichael, Gladys Aylward, Jim Elliot, Elka of the Wai Wai (look that one up!), and Lesslie Newbigin, to name a few. It was the power of the Word that grabbed hold of these missionaries' hearts and revolutionized their actions, leading to transformed people groups and nations.

 ## Savor the Beauty

We might not always think of Bible study as being "delightful," but its practice is key to helping us "delight in God" and align with his ways.

Psalm 37:4 is an invitation to "delight yourself in the Lord, and he will give you the desires of your heart" (ESV).[2] This verse can be quoted almost as a bargaining chip for prosperity, where people list their desires and hope they can take advantage of this promise. But what if we approached this verse differently? What if we considered that we don't really know the deepest desires of our hearts, but God does? What if we saw the opportunity to "delight" in him as a chance to align our hearts with the desires he has put within us—our deepest desires that are fulfilled in him?

---

2   This passage was the catalytic prompt that led us to write this book.

The beauty of God is infinite; we cannot possibly fathom just how delightful he is. There is no end to his perfection. To study Scripture in such a way that we see more of the beauty of God is an invaluable practice.

Practice

Either by audio, reading, or through exegetical study of a passage, invest in time studying the Word. You may want to read Psalms 1, 19, and 119 for this day to prepare your heart to receive well from God. There are several ways you can approach studying the Bible. Prayerfully ask God what he is leading you to focus on. You could choose to study through a theme, such as worship, priesthood, or shepherding. Or perhaps you might decide to read through one book of the Bible. (If you're unsure of what to pick, try a shorter book, such as Ephesians or Philippians.) You can even conduct a broader study on particular types of biblical literature, such as the Law, prophetic literature, or apocalyptic literature. Of course, a big part of Bible study is engaging with the text, either by reading or listening to it, but don't forget to look at resources available through books, podcasts, online teaching, and apps. You may want to look at a few different perspectives on a passage and read or listen to it in some different translations of the Bible to see what God may reveal to you.

If Bible study is difficult for you, remember these practices are not to earn God's favor or to achieve a sense of self-righteousness. Ask the Lord to bring you into the joy of communion with him through this practice, so that you may perceive him in renewed ways.

After you have experienced this practice, consider what resources you might need that will help you with this practice. Is there a group you could join, or are there others in your Christian community who might benefit from exploring this practice together? Although there is a time and place for reading large portions of Scripture quickly, it's important to take your time to study. If you decide to work through a book in the Bible, give yourself sufficient time to go slowly and thoroughly. This could take a few months or even a year if it is very in-depth.

Key Resources

- Psalms 1; 19; 119.

- Kenneth Boa, *Conformed to His Image: Biblical, Practical Approaches to Spiritual Formation* (Zondervan Academic, 2020). Although this book is comprehensive concerning all areas of spiritual growth, Boa has many sections dealing specifically with resources for studying the Word diligently and devotionally.

- D. A. Carson (ed.), *The Enduring Authority of the Christian Scriptures* (Apollos, 2016). For those who want a more academic exploration of the historical, theological, epistemological, and world religion-related issues pertaining to the authority of Scripture, we recommend this massive resource. Though quite academic in approach, it offers an incredibly coherent and sound collection of highly intellectual arguments for the authority of Scripture. Just for fun, take a look at the table of contents for this book on its Amazon page.

- Gordon D. Fee and Douglas Stuart, *How to Read the Bible for All Its Worth* and *How to Read the Bible Book by Book: A Guided Tour* (Zondervan Academic, 2014). Both of these books focus on hermeneutics, genre analysis, and learning background information relevant to equipping the reader to be a sound student of Scripture.

- Howard G. Hendricks and William D. Hendricks, *Living by the Book: The Art and Science of Reading the Bible* (Moody Publishers, 2007).

- *The Bible Project*, https://bibleproject.com/. This is an excellent resource for studying themes throughout the Bible. It is available through a website and as an app, with lots of videos, podcasts, and written resources to help you (or a small group) study the Bible.

- *Third Mill*, https://thirdmill.org/. This is a ministry that has taken some of the best seminary courses from several of the top theology and Bible professors around the world and offers it completely free on their site. Their goal is to provide the best biblical and theological education to those who cannot afford seminary fees.

- Oletta Wald, *The Joy of Discovery in Bible Study* (Augsburg Fortress, 2002).

Soaking Prayer

Purpose

To learn how to let God's presence minister to us. To learn how to slow down and still the heart, soul, mind, and body before the Lord, while giving space for him to minister through music and rest in him.

Go Deeper

Much can be learned from both the charismatic and contemplative movements. There isn't time to go into their rich histories here, but each movement brings with it great benefits as well as some imbalances. Exploring spiritual practices incorporating the perspectives of both "Spirit-oriented" and "contemplative" believers provides valuable insights as we learn how to draw near to the Lord. Soaking prayer isn't dissimilar from silence and solitude, but it typically includes music and a structured use of the time. Think of soaking prayer as an opportunity to learn how to rest in the Lord (Ps. 37:7), to wait patiently on him (Ps. 40:1–2), and to long and thirst for him (Ps. 42:1).

A standard time of soaking prayer looks like finding a quiet place, taking fifteen to thirty minutes to play some worship music, and simply relaxing in God's presence. Lying down while the music is playing allows us to physically posture ourselves before the Lord in a way that says, "I am here, resting in your presence." Focus on his presence with you and how he wants to reveal more of his love to you. If something comes up in your mind or heart during this time, write it down and return to it later, then refocus on the Lord (unless it is evident that you need to change gears and deal with the issue). Let this be a time to rest, fully trusting in him.

Missional Spirituality

As missional disciples, we are often in danger of being so busy and following God's calling on our lives that we forget Jesus' words that his yoke is easy, and his burden is light (Matt. 11:30). Jesus calls us to come to him and get the rest we need. Soaking prayer is a perfect way to find that rest. Sometimes we might even fall asleep during this time—that's a good thing! We are allowing ourselves to rest like a child in our loving Father's embrace. Here we get to receive and rest instead of constantly striving to be purposeful. Monica and I have found doing this several times a month significantly blesses us, enriches our faith more deeply, and helps us to stop the frenetic cycles we get into when we are busy "on mission."

In testifying to God's power in their lives, eighteenth-century revivalist leaders John Wesley and George Whitefield both noted moments, or critical turning points, when they experienced a complete life change as the power of God flowed through them. These turning points arose after significant times of prayer, including soaking in the presence of the Lord for long periods of time. Keep in mind these two historic "missional practitioners" were on disparate ends of some theological debates, yet they both experienced the transformative power of God via soaking in his presence. Both also claimed their ministries increased significantly *after* these times.[1]

The famous Welsh evangelist Christmas Evans, who ministered at the turn of the nineteenth century, exemplified the power of prayerful soaking in the presence of God.[2] Evans found himself mired in schisms regarding doctrinal debates of the day and felt his heart growing cold and weary. He prayed and spent time in the presence of the Lord until finally he "felt as if the shackles were falling off and as if the mountains

---

1 James Gilchrest Lawson, *Deeper Experiences of Famous Christians*, 3rd ed., abridged (Warner Press, 2007), 63.
2 Although his soaking wasn't the same in form as we are speaking of here, it was, however, the same in function: he spent substantial time before the Lord waiting for an inner transformation regarding his "cold heart."

of snow and ice were melting within" him.[3] Describing his experience, he says: "I felt my whole spirit relieved of some great bondage, and as if it were rising up from the grave of a severe winter. My tears flowed copiously and I was constrained to cry aloud and pray for the gracious visits of God, for the joy of His salvation."[4] Sometimes simply resting in God's presence and submitting to his work (without any obvious effort from us) allows us to experience deep and personal breakthroughs.

Savor the Beauty

Of all the practices we have covered so far, soaking prayer is one of the more notable ways to connect with the beauty of God. Monica and I have participated in communal soaking times, where people engaged in soaking prayer together and then shared what the Lord was doing in their hearts. Each time, people would share their revelation that God is more caring, loving, gentle, good, and kind than they could have imagined.

Practice

Find a place to lie down where you can be comfortable and uninterrupted. Play some worship music and invite God's presence. This soaking practice is a bit like sunbathing, where you feel like your body is "soaking up" the heat from the sun. This is a time to allow yourself to rest with the Lord. Let God use the music to minister and speak to you. Most people do this practice for at least thirty minutes, but you can be in this space as long as you need. If you find your mind wandering, redirect your focus back to God and invite his presence.

Some people use worship music, others use instrumental music, and others turn out the lights and lay in the dark to help them focus. Experiment and see what works best for you. Once you have finished, journal your encounter with God. Did he say anything specific to you? Did he give you any reassurances? How did you encounter his presence? Has something in you changed as a result of your intentional time with him? Consider how you could incorporate this practice into your practices as a church, small group, or Christian community. Are there times in your week when

---

3 Quoted by Gilchrest Lawson in *Deeper Experiences of Famous Christians*, 87. (This booklet is tiny, but has an incredible list of people who have encountered the Lord in powerful ways throughout history.)
4 Ibid.

you look for alternate ways to "rest" (e.g., TV, social media scrolling, reading, going to the gym) that you could replace with soaking prayer instead?

Key Resources

- Psalms 37:7; 40:1–2; 42:1; 84.

- Lamentations 3:21–26.

  Although these don't directly discuss soaking prayer, the following are implicitly helpful and focus on the heart of worship:

- Randy Alcorn, *Heaven* (Tyndale Momentum, 2004).

- Jonathan Edwards, *The End for Which God Created the World* (CreateSpace, 2014).

- J. I. Packer, *Knowing God* (IVP, 1973).

- Edward Pearse, *A Beam of Divine Glory: The Unchangeableness of God* (Soli Deo Gloria Ministries, 2003).

- John Piper, *Desiring God: Meditations of a Christian Hedonist* (Blackstone, 2006).

- Allen P. Ross, *Recalling the Hope of Glory: Biblical Worship from the Garden to the New Creation* (Kregel Academic & Professional, 2006). This is an exceptional and comprehensive theological treatment of worship.

- A. W. Tozer, *The Pursuit of God* (Christian Publications, Inc., 1948).

Act of Kindness,
Act of Generosity

Purpose
To live out of the abundance God has given us and bless others, through both kindness and generosity.

Go Deeper
We often make the bar too high for how we measure our ministry or service to others, thinking we need to do something flashy and amazing for it to "count." However, simple acts such as buying someone a meal, spending time with someone who is lonely, calling a friend, or helping out with a household chore can have a much bigger impact than we think. Small acts amount to large effects in the kingdom of heaven. Jesus spoke of the kingdom being like seeds scattered or yeast worked into dough (Matt. 13:31–33). He used these parabolic metaphors of small things having greater value than their size would imply. The kingdom of heaven can be found in small, creative acts of love toward others.

In Psalm 50, God states he owns all the cattle and birds, and he has incredible resources completely at his disposal. Jesus also demonstrated this abundance when he took the fish and bread and fed the multitudes (Matt. 14, 15; Mark 8; John 6). If our God, who has all the resources imaginable at his disposal, is the One who takes care of us, we don't have to worry about holding on to things for ourselves. We can be generous to others through deeds of kindness and through sharing the resources given to us by God. These practices may seem small and simple, but they reveal what's in our hearts about whom we are trusting to care for us. Do we trust in our own abilities and resources? Or are we aware that all we have is already a gift to us and so we can give to others out of what we have received?

Missional Spirituality

What witness is there without love? What witness is there without deeds that back up the claimed values of the doer? We can talk all day about generosity, but until people see tangible acts of love, they won't know we are sincere. The saying goes, "Actions speak louder than words." An action can clearly and potently communicate a significant amount of our beliefs, values, and convictions without requiring words. In mission, we must demonstrate the love of God and the coming of his kingdom, as well as share words of his good news. Our words must be full of life, love, and wisdom, but our actions must demonstrate character and integrity to back up our words.

Sometimes a simple act of love can have an enormous impact on transforming someone's life. An acquaintance who was angry toward Christians once invited Jeremy and me to celebrate a special event with them, and so we brought them a gift. It was something simple, but it changed how they interacted with us from that moment on. A friendship was formed, catalyzed by that small act of kindness and generosity. The gift created a doorway for relationship because that person felt loved. We can never fully predict the impact of a simple act—a smile, a $3 gift, or a small act of service can make all the difference and change the entire dynamic of a relationship.

Savor the Beauty

Small acts of kindness change the giver as well as the recipient. Pay attention to how it makes you feel. Does your heart or soul resound in any way with this deed? You may find that an act of kindness is more deeply healing for you than you had initially recognized. Over the centuries, many theologians have noted the joy a kind gesture can bring to the giver.[1] Actions of love and kindness help us to see more of the goodness of God; we begin to identify with him in his desire to pour out his love on all his people.

Practice

At the beginning of your day, consider someone you could be kind and generous to. What act could express that kindness, and how could it be a sacrificial act of generosity? You may even want to plan more than one deed. Intentionality makes all the difference. You are training yourself to rediscover the lost art of kindness. Create an opportunity today to bless someone else by giving sacrificially from your own resources. Perhaps spend some time praying to see if God brings a particular person to mind to whom you could be generous.

After you have experienced this practice, perhaps take some time to review your resources, thank God for his generosity toward you, and prayerfully consider how you could be more generous with what you have.

---

1 See the writings of Augustine, C. S. Lewis, and Dallas Willard in particular.

Key Resources

- Colossians 3:12–17.

- Matthew 22:37–39.

- John 12:26.

- Romans 12:3–21.

- Randy Alcorn, *The Treasure Principle: Unlocking the Secret of Joyful Giving* (Multnomah Books, 2005).

- Our book, *Kingdom Contours*, includes thoughtful theory and tools for loving neighbors well and generously. See chapter three, "Incarnational Living." Jeremy and Monica Chambers, *Kingdom Contours: Empowering Everyday People With the Tools to Shape Kingdom Movements* (Missional Challenge, 2020).

- Larry Crabb, *Encouragement: The Unexpected Power of Building Others Up* (Zondervan, 2013).

- Timothy Keller, *The Freedom of Self Forgetfulness: The Path to True Christian Joy* (10Publishing, 2012). This is a tiny but potent book on the idea of losing our self-obsession and discovering a deeper life filled with passion for the Lord. This directly correlates to our ability to also love our neighbor without ourselves in view.

- James Bryan Smith, *The Good and Beautiful Community: Following the Spirit, Extending Grace, Demonstrating Love* (IVP, 2010). Excellent for intentional practices concerning community and kindness.

Intercessory Prayer

Purpose

To join the Spirit and Christ in interceding for others, discover the friendship of having Jesus with us when we lift up others to God, and align our hearts with the heartbeat of the Father.

Go Deeper

Intercessory prayer should be a regular practice in the lives of followers of Jesus. After all, we are told to pray without ceasing (1 Thess. 5:16–18), to let our requests be made known before the Lord (Phil. 4:6), and to pray with all supplication (Eph. 6:18). Scripture often invites us to join in with the Lord's work via prayer. We are told that Jesus is our Advocate (1 John 2:1) and that the Spirit intercedes for us (Rom. 8:26–27), and we are invited and instructed to enter into this heavenly work.

Today, take extra time to practice the intercessory approach. This means to wait on the Lord, discern whom he has laid on your heart, and lift them up in prayer.

A word of caution: this is not the time to obsess over the sins or issues of those we love, but rather it is a time to lift them to the Lord, asking for grace, joy, love, and his blessing upon them. If we pray without love, it is merely a noisy prayer (1 Cor. 13).

Often when our prayer time is full of complaints or focusing on the faults of others, we are not keeping our prayers in line with the fruit of the Spirit. There is a place for lament, but there is a difference between lament and complaint; the key is trust. As we intercede, we choose to deeply trust God, enabling our hearts to rejoice with the work the Lord is doing. Keep it simple: focus on lifting others up to God so you may join in with the good intentions the Lord has for them!

Jeremy and I have typically noticed that when we begin intercessory prayer, there is an initial phase when we surrender to God our own desires for the person, and ask him to give us *his* perspective. If there is hurt or offense in our hearts, we give this to the Father and ask for his strength to forgive. Then we are able to pray God's best for the other person. *To love someone is to will the best for them.* This means our prayers must come to a point where we want this person to experience the absolute *best* thing they could ever experience, which is a transformative experience of God. As we practice intercessory prayer, we move into deeper trust and surrender to God, remembering that he is in control.

Below is a selection of some of the excellent prayers the apostle Paul communicated through his letters.[1] Look at some of these prayers and consider Paul's values and how he prayed so specifically in his intercession for the churches:

> *And it is my prayer that your love may abound more and more, with knowledge and all discernment, so that you may approve what is excellent, and so be pure and blameless for the day of Christ, filled with the fruit of righteousness that comes through Jesus Christ, to the glory and praise of God.*
>
> PHILIPPIANS 1:9–11

> *And so, from the day we heard, we have not ceased to pray for you, asking that you may be filled with the knowledge of his will in all spiritual wisdom and understanding, so as to walk in a manner worthy of the Lord, fully pleasing to him: bearing fruit in every good*

1　D. A. Carson, in his excellent book *Praying with Paul*, discusses these passages and many more. The aim of his book is to help the reader learn from Paul's praying style in order to pray more for the things of eternal value and to adopt the same mentality Paul demonstrated through his prayers. The book encourages us to ask questions such as, "For someone to pray this way, what does that say about the person and their values?" or "What kind of person would actually pray this way? And what kind of belief system is required for someone to desire to pray in such a way?" The answers to these questions will have a profound impact. See D. A. Carson, *Praying with Paul: A Call to Spiritual Reformation* (Baker Academic, 2015).

work and increasing in the knowledge of God; being strengthened with all power, according to his glorious might, for all endurance and patience with joy.

COLOSSIANS 1:9–11

Now may the God of peace himself sanctify you completely, and may your whole spirit and soul and body be kept blameless at the coming of our Lord Jesus Christ. He who calls you is faithful; he will surely do it.

1 THESSALONIANS 5:23–24

For this reason I bow my knees before the Father, from whom every family in heaven and on earth is named, that according to the riches of his glory he may grant you to be strengthened with power through his Spirit in your inner being, so that Christ may dwell in your hearts through faith—that you, being rooted and grounded in love, may have strength to comprehend with all the saints what is the breadth and length and height and depth, and to know the love of Christ that surpasses knowledge, that you may be filled with all the fullness of God. Now to him who is able to do far more abundantly than all that we ask or think, according to the power at work within us, to him be glory in the church and in Christ Jesus throughout all generations, forever and ever. Amen.

EPHESIANS 3:14–21

Consider also the intercession of Jesus in John 17. You may want to read and pray the entire passage to the Lord.

Missional Spirituality

Over the years, Jeremy and I have interviewed over three hundred older missionaries, ministry leaders, theology professors, and other godly believers with specific questions about what they have learned in their faith journey. The answers from these interviews yielded similar patterns. Toward the end of their lives, these godly believers commented that even though they were unable to do their former "ministry," they were now interceding more diligently and intensely for others than ever before. So the thought hit us one day: why wait until we are older to begin this sort of prayer life? Why not begin practicing now? If so many older godly folk describe their lives as culminating in a lifestyle of intercessory prayer, then why not plunge into the depths of this now, in the earlier decades of our lives?

Many missionaries over the centuries have also noted that the best ministry springs out of a prayerful life: stepping into the place of praying on behalf of others, wrestling against spiritual forces of wickedness, and moving into a place of intercession.[2] Such prayer aligns our hearts with God's; it brings us to a place of humility and surrender. We are reminded that God loves and cares for people more than we do. As we surrender, our interactions with those to whom we are ministering change from a posture of fixing or saving to one of open hands, trusting that God is the One who is doing the work and is lovingly allowing us to be a part of it. Prayer opens our eyes to see the things God is doing that perhaps we wouldn't have seen otherwise. He is at work, with or without us, and he often reveals this to us through prayer. We must remember that our work is not merely physical but also spiritual. There is far more going on with the people we are interacting with than we could know. So we come with prayerful humility before God, asking him to do the spiritual work and bring the freedom that only he can bring.

Locally and globally, Jeremy and I have seen unusual, surprising, and even mind-boggling answers to intercessory prayers. We have seen things that cannot be attributed to nature or chance but instead can only be the direct answers to prayers in absolutely miraculous ways.

 ## Savor the Beauty

In true intercession we also become attentive to the heart of the Lord. We sense his love for others and us. We learn what grieves him and what makes him rejoice. Intercessory prayer is one way to deepen our union with him. It is a beautiful partnership.

---

2   George Müller is an excellent example of this. His journals revealed how much he prayed faithfully for everything and saw many direct answers to prayers. You can read more about this in *The Autobiography of George Müller* (Whitaker House, 1984).

Practice

Start with silence before God, recognizing his presence and waiting on him. Slow down and ask the Lord to direct your prayer time and enable you to pray in unity with his heart. As people or issues arise in your heart, let your requests be made known (Phil. 4:5–7) and ask in Jesus' name (John 14:13–17). However, ask with a submissive heart, surrendering your requests to his will (1 John 5:14; James 4:7). Come with thanksgiving and humility. Allow yourself to be open to the idea that God may be leading you to act in some way. Many well-known intercessors (such as the Welsh missionary Rees Howells) have shared how their experiences of prayer have led them to actions that allowed God's kingdom to break through in new ways.

After you have experienced this practice, consider how you could keep a prayer journal where you write down the people and situations God is laying on your heart and how he is answering those prayers.

Key Resources

- John 17.

- Roberta Bondi, *To Love as God Loves: Conversations with the Early Church* (Fortress Press, 1987).

- D. A. Carson, *Praying with Paul: A Call to Spiritual Reformation* (Baker Academic, 2015).

- Jim Cymbala, *Fresh Wind, Fresh Fire: What Happens When God's Spirit Invades the Hearts of His People* (Zondervan, 2003).

- Wesley Duewel, *Mighty Prevailing Prayer: Experiencing the Power of Answered Prayer* (Zondervan, 2013).

- Peter Grieg, *Red Moon Rising: How 24-7 Prayer is Awakening a Generation* (Relevant Books, 2003).

- Douglas McKelvey, *Every Moment Holy*, vol. 1 (The Rabbit Room, 2017). This includes a beautiful liturgy, "For Those with a Sudden Burden to Intercede" (p. 173).

- George Müller, *The Autobiography of George Müller* (Whitaker House, 1996).

- Terrance Tiessen, *Providence and Prayer: How Does God Work in the World?* (IVP Academic, 2000). This covers ten views on the involvement of God in this world and how our prayers can be prayed with coherent consistency that aligns with our theology. The reader is encouraged to consider what they believe and then pray accordingly. Although this book is a more philosophical and deeply theological work, it is worth wading through for the student and practitioner of prayer.

- John Wimber and Kevin Springer, *Power Evangelism* (Chosen Books, 2009). This book shares some powerful testimonies from the Vineyard movement. It may be stretching for those who don't come from charismatic backgrounds, but it is a must-read.

Practicing His Presence

Purpose

To train ourselves to be continually conscious of the truth that Jesus is with us in *every detail and moment of the day,* and we can live life with him, moment by moment, finding his presence to be all that we need.

Go Deeper

The idea here is to remove the false divide between the sacred and secular. We can easily fall into the trap of assuming that some things are spiritual (sacred), and others are not (secular). Many of us are only able to see God's hand at work when we are worshiping, praying, or spending specific time focused on him. But when we lean into the practice of knowing God's presence in everything, all elements of our day can be considered spiritual and consecrated unto him. The Scriptures wouldn't tell us to "pray without ceasing" (1 Thess. 5:17) if there wasn't a dynamic way of entering into an honorable observation of that command. It is quite possible to allow our days and our moments to become consumed by his presence and reality. This doesn't mean we are praying 24/7 with our eyes closed and hands together, but rather that we walk with him alongside us, we talk with his thoughts in our mind, and we become increasingly aware of his presence. We share a constant communion.

Brother Lawrence, Frank Laubach, Thomas Kelly, and Richard Foster have all written about constantly abiding in the presence of the Lord, moment by moment.[1] This might seem particularly challenging in our age of distraction where, in the form of a smartphone, we carry the entire world everywhere we go. But instead of being intimidated by this practice, we can begin with small steps, such as asking God to make himself obvious to us throughout our day.

As Jeremy and I mentioned in the contemplative prayer practice (see pages 51–56), God is more real than anything we can imagine. When we practice his presence, we acknowledge that he is there with us, just as he promised he would be (2 Cor. 6:16). We start to see God as a partner alongside us in our spiritual pilgrimage in this life. He becomes a close companion (one whom we are now taking more notice of). As we inwardly turn our attention to him, there is comfort and peace. There have been many times when I (Monica) have turned my attention to God's presence with me, and I felt the entire moment change. For example, I've experienced peace when encountering a person I find difficult, seeing them through the lens of God's love.

Missional Spirituality

Jeremy and I have noticed that intentionally practicing God's presence is profoundly beneficial while on mission. The sudden remembrance of his presence has allowed us to calm down and rethink stressful situations. In many of the tiny details of a typical day, the acute awareness that Jesus is literally there with us changes how we approach these moments. Mission becomes an overflow of his presence: you become "presence driven." Frantic mission is no true mission, but mission alongside Jesus is more enjoyable and powerful than we can imagine.

Savor the Beauty

When we spend our day being aware of God's presence, we begin to notice more of his beauty. And to see the beauty of God all day is transformative. If we look for the Lord in all moments of the day, we see how prevalent he is. Take this day to return as often as possible to the awareness that

---

1   It should also be noted that each of these authors, in their accounts of "practicing the presence of God," testified that after periods of time invested in this practice, they experienced incredibly overwhelming assurance of God's presence, as well as euphoria and ecstatic bliss of connecting so deeply with the Lord. They weren't "seeking experiences"—they were seeking the Lord, but they also all experienced deep, soul-impacting rewards from this practice.

he is with you always, even until the end of the age (Matt. 28:20). Remember this is a practice! It doesn't have to be done perfectly. As our friends in the Renovaré Institute often say, "Do as you can, not as you can't"—meaning that you just keep practicing walking with the Lord. Don't let perfection be the enemy of the delightful.

When we take this practice seriously, we will begin to notice small things, such as flowers, a delicious bite of food, the smile on the face of a friend, or a brief stressful moment that is redeemed by the grace of the Lord. The eighteenth-century preacher Jonathan Edwards spoke of this being like having a "new sense"—we suddenly look around us and the fundamental nature of reality appears different. Now it is imbued with glory and goodness from the Lord for us to savor and enjoy! Consider the difference this could make with our struggles if we would simply learn to turn our eyes upon Jesus more throughout our days.

Practice

You can practice God's presence in many different ways, so find an application that works best for you. You may want to set an alarm every hour (or more frequently) to remind you to pause and recognize that God is with you. You could set visible reminders around your house or office, prompting you to pause and be aware of his loving presence periodically throughout the day; or you could put something in your pocket that reminds you to turn your attention back to the Lord. You may want to say short prayers while you are engaged in a particular task, such as putting on your shoes, brushing your teeth, or washing the dishes. The key is discovering what works for you and your schedule, so you train yourself to be aware of his presence, moment by moment. This deliberate act of diligent pursuit of the Lord can change everything in your life.

After you have experienced this practice, perhaps you could spend a particular day each week engaging more intentionally with this practice and then see if it could spill over into the other days of your week.

Key Resources

- John 15:4–11.

- 1 Thessalonians 5:16–18.

- Kenneth Boa, *Conformed to His Image: Biblical, Practical Approaches to Spiritual Formation* (Zondervan Academic, 2020). All of the chapters pertaining to prayer are relevant to this practice.

- D. A. Carson, *Praying with Paul: A Call to Spiritual Reformation* (Baker Academic, 2015).

- Jim Cymbala with Dean Merrill, *Fresh Wind, Fresh Fire: What Happens When God's Spirit Invades the Hearts of His People* (Zondervan, 2003).

- Wesley L. Duewel, *Mighty Prevailing Prayer: Experiencing the Power of Answered Prayer* (Zondervan, 2013).

- François Fénelon, *Christian Perfection* (Harper & Row, 1947) and *Maxims of the Mystics* (Mowbray, 1909).

- Richard Foster, *Prayer: Finding the Heart's True Home* (HarperOne, 2002).

- Richard Foster, *Sanctuary of the Soul: A Journey Into Meditative Prayer* (Hodder & Stoughton, 2012).

- Brother Lawrence, *The Practice of the Presence of God: Being Conversations and Letters of Nicholas Herman of Lorraine (Brother Lawrence)* (Martino Fine Books, 2016).

- Brother Lawrence and Frank Laubach, *Practicing His Presence* (Christian Books Pub House, 1973).

- Saint Teresa of Avila, *The Interior Castle* (Tan Books, 2011).

Worship Music

Purpose

To allow song and music to be a catalyst for the renewing of our minds, the reviving of our hearts, and the restoring of our souls, moving us into deeper intimacy with the Lord.

Go Deeper

It is incredible how spending time in worship can change the nature of our entire day. Sometimes we might not have time to practice musical or sung worship ourselves, but we can easily listen to worship music while we are engaged in other activities. Let worship be the soundtrack to our days. Psalms 95, 100, 103, and 145 are all excellent psalms to turn to when engaging in this practice. They exhort us to praise the Lord and to reflect upon his goodness. Our minds and hearts are prone to wander, but if we allow worship to direct the flow of our attention throughout the day, it makes an amazing difference.

Missional Spirituality

Monica and I once felt the Lord calling us to go on a beach trip with some friends who were engaging in destructive habits with drastic consequences.[1] Our friends were slowly destroying themselves due to their hatred of themselves and others. During our time away together, we were deeply saddened to see the extent of the pain in their lives. We tried to share some of God's good news with them, but they were not in a place to receive it.

Late one night, when we were wracked with grief for our friends, we went out for a walk by ourselves. In the distance we could hear music … *worship* music. Without saying a word or even glancing at each other, we immediately began walking toward the faint music, as if a pied piper was leading us. Although the stars were shining beautifully, it was pitch black, but we kept moving toward the music until we were about fifty yards away. We sat down and both started crying tears of joy as we praised the Lord. The music reminded us of who God is and strengthened our faith to persevere and cling to him.

We wanted to thank the people playing the music, so we approached them, but we were so emotional we couldn't even say "thank you" loudly enough! Startled, they turned down the music, asking us to repeat what we said. After thanking them again, we had a great conversation where we were able to share with them how much the worship blessed us. This experience enabled us to return to our friends with deeper love and hope from the Lord in our hearts.

John and Charles Wesley, two men who launched a missional movement that has impacted countless people and many nations, both had a deep passion for singing worship and songwriting. It was a discipline and practice they held to throughout their lives, and many of the all-time most famous hymns are attributed to the two of them. Perhaps the practice of writing and singing helped fuel their commitment to the Lord and enabled them to engage deeply with his heart while walking on mission. Worship can kickstart mission and rejuvenate the weary pilgrim, providing them the strength to continue.

Savor the Beauty

Our experience of the worship we came across that night can be summed up with the words from the hymn, *Heaven Came Down:*[2]

---

1 Some details have been changed for the sake of confidentiality.
2 John W. Peterson. "Heaven Came Down," 1961, John W. Peterson Music Company. Used by permission.

O what a wonderful, wonderful day—day I will never forget;

After I'd wandered in darkness away, Jesus my Savior I met.

O what a tender, compassionate friend—He met the need of my heart;

Shadows dispelling, With joy I am telling, He made all the darkness depart.

Heaven came down and glory filled my soul,

When at the cross the Savior made me whole;

My sins were washed away—

And my night was turned to day—

Heaven came down and glory filled my soul!

Born of the Spirit with life from above into God's fam'ly divine,

Justified fully thru Calvary's love, O what a standing is mine!

And the transaction so quickly was made when as a sinner I came,

Took of the offer of grace He did proffer—He saved me, O praise His dear name!

Now I've a hope that will surely endure after the passing of time;

I have a future in heaven for sure, there in those mansions sublime.

And it's because of that wonderful day when at the cross I believed;

Riches eternal and blessings supernal from His precious hand I received.[3]

Practice

Play worship music of any genre of your choosing as much as you can throughout the day. If you enjoy playing worship music with an instrument, singing along, or even writing your own songs, spend some time worshiping in this way.

After you have experienced this practice, perhaps you could consider setting your alarm to play worship music, listening to worship during breakfast, or playing it on your commute. You could make a playlist that you can return to or pick your favorite worship albums, so they are ready whenever you have the opportunity to worship.

---

3 We pray our friends we went on a beach trip with can someday joyfully sing this song.

Key Resources

- John 4:24.

- Hebrews 12:28–29.

- Revelation 4:11.

- Randy Alcorn, *Heaven* (Tyndale Momentum, 2004).

- Hymnals—pick up any older hymnal and read through the songs; note the ones that move your heart to worship.

- J. I. Packer, *Knowing God* (IVP, 1973).

- John Piper, *Desiring God: Meditations of a Christian Hedonist* (Blackstone, 2006).

- Allen P. Ross, *Recalling the Hope of Glory: Biblical Worship from the Garden to the New Creation* (Kregel Academic & Professional, 2006). This is an exceptional and exhaustive theological treatment of worship.

- A. W. Tozer, *The Pursuit of God* (Christian Publications, Inc., 1948).

- The writings of the Puritans. See https://www.theheritage.blog/blog/the-ultimate-puritan-reading-list.

- YouTube—browse playlists on YouTube or elsewhere that include specific genres of worship. Try exploring beyond your normal genre of choice in worship: many Christian artists have written incredible worshipful songs that would not typically be considered "worship music" yet are spiritually deep.

Nature

Purpose

To observe creative beauty and wisdom. To discover how nature reveals the genius of God and, by observing his artwork, we honor him.

Go Deeper

We interact with God's creation more than most of us realize. If you have a pet, that is creation. Your family members are the creation of God. When you breathe air, that is his creation. Your body is his creation. Have you ever stopped and looked at your hands or any part of your body and said, "Wow, God. You made this!"? Try it. Every single time you eat, you are eating either his direct creation or something that is based on things he made. Have you ever stopped and looked at a banana? Consider the peel, the smell, the taste, the texture—all of these were designed by God to be this way. We interact with God's creation far more than we may realize. If only we kept this awareness constant in our lives!

Today's practice is a tangible application of the biblical command, "In all your ways acknowledge him" (Prov. 3:6 ESV). We get to know God better by paying attention to his creative genius as displayed in his creation. So in all our ways, in our breathing, our bodies, our eating, our friends, our families, our pets, our time outside

... *acknowledge him.* Some people have a hard time getting their minds focused on the Lord. But if we allow nature to be a constant reminder of him, we suddenly have a spiritual prompt everywhere we go.

Missional Spirituality

Consider Jesus, the quintessential missionary. He traveled into his own creation and became flesh so he could minister and proclaim his kingdom to this world. He walked everywhere with his followers, and they spent significant amounts of time outside, seeing the very things Jesus made. His words and parables often involved his creation.

Allowing God to speak to us through his creation can restore us for the work of mission, as well as being a way to connect those we are reaching to the Lord as Creator.

God ministers to me (Monica) significantly through nature. There have been many times when ministry and mission have felt heavy or difficult to bear. The Lord has led me to walk on trails where I am reminded of his presence and receive his peace. He realigns my perspective through the magnitude of all the creation around me. Creation does not strive to survive but instead is held up and cared for by God himself. As Jesus says in Matthew 6, if God can care for the trees and plants and everything else around me, how much more does he care for me and those to whom I am ministering?

Nature is also an incredibly powerful witness. To take people into nature is to take them into a possible connection with God; it is to expose them to the place where creation screams out his glory.

Savor the Beauty

We study the Word because we value what God has communicated so clearly; yet many of us forget to study nature, through which God also communicates to us (Rom. 1:20). Some call this a sacramental view of reality, recognizing that God has deposited some of his creative goodness and wisdom into everything he has made, and therefore *everything* he has made is worth our attention and contemplation. Even watching a documentary on some natural phenomenon (such as volcanoes or lightning) can cause us to pause in absolute wonder at God's power. Or spending time near still water can make us aware of his peace. If we ever doubt God's goodness, getting out into nature can remind us of his provision and care.

In 2020, Monica and I chose to live on the fourteenth floor of an apartment building overlooking the James River in Richmond, VA. We moved there specifically because of the heavenly views from the balcony, which provoked us to deeper worship. We quickly discovered our balcony also had an unusual number of spiders, so we even learned to worship the Lord by watching the spiders build webs and eat little insects. Two years later we moved to Denver, CO, in part to fulfill the mission God had called us to but also to respond to his invitation to worship him in nature (and to take others to worship him there as well).

When we take groups on spiritual retreats, we frequently go out into nature to look for an object that illustrates a spiritual principle the Lord is teaching us, or we encourage the group to spend some time sitting in nature considering creation as God's art form, contemplating what it reveals about God. Our groups return enriched and revived. Some are reminded that God has everything in control and is good and trustworthy, while others encounter a greater depth of God's love.

Philosopher Dallas Willard regularly told a story of a sunset on a beach in Cape Town, South Africa. As he watched the sunset it occurred to him that God must be an infinitely happy God because he gets to see every sunset on every planet constantly (as the sun is constantly "setting" somewhere). Think of the beauty that God enjoys, and think of how much God invites you to join in on savoring the beauty of his creation with him!

Practice

Find a way to engage with the natural world today. This could be by sitting outside, going for a walk, driving through an area of natural beauty, or visiting a place where you can get close to God's creation. You can also do this by staying indoors and enjoying a plant, animal, fruit, or vegetable, watching a nature documentary, or stargazing through your window. As you do this practice, ask yourself, "What type of God would make this creative beauty?" Today, make it your aim to reflect on what his creation reveals about him.

After you have experienced this practice, consider what places, people, and things help you see the beauty of God through his creation, and how you could bring more of those into your life. You might want to take up a new hobby that gets you outside more or try to grow something yourself at home. How could this practice become part of what you do in your Christian community—perhaps by sharing a garden, taking time to worship outside, or by thanking God for his creation when you eat meals together?

Key Resources

- Genesis 1:29, 31; 2:15.

- Psalms 19; 24:1–2.

- G. K. Chesterton, *Orthodoxy* (Ignatius Press, 1995). This is a profound and thoughtful examination of the beauty of God displayed in nature. Chesterton uses the term "magical" to describe the universe as having meaning, which, for him, is the direct implication of the intention of God as the Divine artist behind all creation.

- Annie Dillard, *Pilgrim at Tinker Creek* (Harper Perennial Modern Classics, 2013). (Eugene Peterson said that Dillard was an "exegete of creation just as John Calvin was an exegete of Scripture." See Eugene H. Peterson, *The Contemplative Pastor: Returning to the Art of Spiritual Direction* [Eerdmans, 1993].)

- Thomas Dubay, *The Evidential Power of Beauty: Science and Theology Meet* (Ignatius Press, 1999).

- Saint Francis of Assisi. Read about the life of Saint Francis, who connected with God through nature in amazing ways. The Wikipedia page provides a great starting point: https://en.wikipedia.org/wiki/Francis_of_Assisi.

Praying the Hours

Purpose

To set moments of refocusing the heart and mind on the Lord throughout the day. To specifically structure the flow of our days around rhythmic and anticipated connection with the Lord.

Go Deeper

Throughout history, people of prayer have discovered that the practice of returning regularly to a prayer ritual or pattern has a powerful impact on the one who prays. For some, this has involved praying at set hours of the day, while for others this has looked like praying at certain intervals rather than each hour. Today's practice is usually based on set prayers, liturgy, or Scriptures. Creating a rhythm or flow to our schedule that is oriented around intimacy with the Lord or theological principles that renew the mind is powerful. These prayers draw our attention back to the Lord. They help us have the words to communicate to him specific requests and longings and give us perspectives we may not have otherwise had. For example, in our evening prayers before bed, Jeremy and I weren't accustomed to asking God to be with "All who are sleeping in this dwelling." But practicing this prayer helped our minds, hearts, and spirits fall asleep better, knowing the embrace of the Lord. Daniel 6:10–28 is an excellent example of a daily rhythm of seeking the Lord. Daniel was so accustomed to intimacy with God that he was willing to risk his life to continue walking in his devotion.

Missional Spirituality

To pause and regain a spiritual perspective three times a day enables us to keep perspective on what we are doing and whom we are called to serve and love. It also allows our day to be structured by prayer rather than whatever our schedule may try to make us prioritize.

We did these prayers daily through the 2020 pandemic, and it was an incredibly enriching practice. Even in the midst of fear-inducing events, such as the urban violence that escalated in Richmond, these prayers reminded us every day that we belong to only one King and one kingdom. As we look back on that time, we believe our deeper rootedness in Christ gave us a greater capacity to love our neighbors, love our city, and care for others. Sure, we didn't do everything right (who did in 2020?), but we are grateful for a year of walking in deeper intimacy with the Lord than we ever had before and being able to walk alongside him in his mission in a more loving way. Despite all the intense hardship we faced during the pandemic, praying the hours helped us to know that God was walking with us through it all.

Monica and I have also practiced these prayer rituals communally.[1] When we've been part of missional communities that chose to corporately do one of the morning, midday, or evening prayers, it became a life-changing rhythm for all those involved. It elevated the quality of each day and unified us as we continued on mission together.

Savor the Beauty

As Jeremy and I lived in this rhythm of daily prayer, we noticed there were times when stressful events would lead us to pause and recite a prayer or reflect on the truth of one of those prayers. When dealing with difficult people or situations we would take a breath and internally pray a line from one of the daily prayers. By regularly reminding ourselves of these truths and

---

1 We've included information here about the Northumbria Community and their daily prayers, which are extremely helpful. In their broader literature, they have some occasionally theologically eccentric points, but in their daily prayers they are trinitarian, insightful, filled with Scripture, and focused on walking with God through every detail of their day.

leaning into God's presence, his beauty became the overarching reality for us. We faced a unique set of trials during 2020 that could have easily caused our year to be devastating (including the death of Jeremy's dad, to whom Jeremy was particularly close). Yet the year was defined by walking closely with God through all the pain and suffering. To experience joy in the midst of so much difficulty is a testament to the supernatural work of God in our lives.[2]

Practice

Stop and pray at set intervals during your day. You can choose to do this several times on the hour, or at specific times, such as morning, noon, and night. Consider using some written prayers or set Scriptures. You may want to use the Celtic prayers of the Northumbria Community.[3] They have morning, midday, and evening prayers that are theologically rich and trinitarian.[4] Or you can create your own prayers specific for different parts of the day, either in your own words or using certain Scriptures. (See some recommended passages in the key resources below.) You may also want to use the *Book of Common Prayer* the Anglican and Episcopal church use.[5]

After you have practiced praying the hours, consider setting aside a specific day of your week when you pray the hours at more frequent intervals. If you are part of a larger household or community, could you incorporate this practice into your rhythm together? The 24-7 Prayer movement has devotional apps for adults and families (Lectio 365 and Lectio for Families—see the Key Resources section at the end of this practice) that in-corporate set prayers and reflections. You might even be able to bring this practice into your workplace.

---

2 Timothy Keller has an excellent book about trials that addresses how we can have an appropriate perspective when we're going through difficulty. See Timothy Keller, *Walking with God through Pain and Suffering* (Hodder & Stoughton, 2013).

3 https://www.northumbriacommunity.org/offices/morning-prayer/.

4 You may also want to get the *Celtic Daily Prayer: Prayers and Readings from the Northumbria Community* (HarperOne, 2002).

5 https://www.churchofengland.org/sites/default/files/2019-10/the-book-of-common-prayer-1662.pdf.

Key Resources

- Psalm 27.

- You could use Psalm 143 for the morning, Psalm 90 for noon, and Psalm 63 for the night.

- Ffald y Brenin, a Welsh prayer movement has a variety of resources: https://ffald-y-brenin.org/prayer#daily-readings.

- Northumbria Community's website: https://www.northumbriacommunity.org/offices/morning-prayer/.

- Northumbria Community, *Celtic Daily Prayer: Prayers and Readings from the Northumbria Community* (HarperOne, 2002).

- The Episcopal Church, *The Book of Common Prayer* (Good Books, 2016). Also see https://www.churchofengland.org/sites/default/files/2019-10/the-book-of-common-prayer-1662.pdf.

- The Moravian daily texts are also scriptural passages and prayers that help you to engage with regular intervals of prayer throughout the day. They have been doing this for hundreds of years! https://www.moravian.org/daily-prayers-for-moravians/.

- 24-7 Prayer's *Lectio 365*, https://www.24-7prayer.com/resource/lectio-365/.

- 24-7 Prayer's *Lectio for Families*, https://www.24-7prayer.com/resource/lectioforfamilies/.

Gratitude

Purpose

To enable the power of gratitude to transform our perspectives and to discover the Lord who is behind all these good gifts.

Go Deeper

In Acts 16:25–26 Paul and Silas are in prison, yet they are still rejoicing and worshiping the Lord. This story illustrates the power of gratitude.

Throughout Scripture there are many examples of people engaging in thanksgiving, as well as exhortations and invitations to be thankful and rejoice in the Lord.[1] It seems to be a powerful action for a believer to practice. Gratitude is extraordinarily effective at changing our perspective and building our faith. It disrupts our compulsions, worries, complaints, pessimism, and conflicts.[2] When we

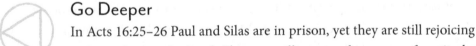

1   See Psalm 51:12; Philippians 4:4; 1 Thessalonians 5:16–17; James 1:2–4; and 1 Peter 1:6–7, to name just a few.

2   We want to be sensitive to the reality that some people suffer with mental health challenges that could create some hurdles for them when seeking to practice gratitude. We are not experts in the field of mental health, and we would always encourage anyone struggling with this to seek appropriate medical support. Although we believe this practice can be beneficial in improving mental health more generally, it should not be used as a substitute for other necessary treatment. We also believe that all of the spiritual practices are designed to encourage and strengthen us in our faith rather than induce guilt if we are struggling with them.

are upset about something, we can notice how our entire demeanor changes when we list a few things we are grateful for to the Lord. If we lived a lifestyle of daily gratitude, it would change everything about our day. We are exhorted in Scripture to be grateful always (1 Thess. 5:16–18) and even told to enter his courts with thanksgiving in our hearts (Psalm 100:4). A true prayer life does not exist without gratitude.

If gratitude is challenging for you, reflect, pray, and consider what the deeper struggle is. Gratitude is hard to force. If your heart is struggling to be thankful, then there may be deeper hurts, bitterness, and conflicts that need to be confronted. Ask the Lord to reveal to you any obstacles that may be preventing gratitude. On the other hand, if gratitude comes easily to you, then consider how you could take it up a notch. Think about how you can allow gratitude to become a daily intentional practice rather than a mere response to good things. Gratitude has to do with perspective, not just circumstances, and the more we cultivate a mind focused on the Lord, the more gratitude will become the prevailing atmosphere of our lives.

Missional Spirituality

Gratitude changes relationships. When we come from a place of expectancy or entitlement, we posture the relationship around what we can get from others, and things become transactional. Missional people minus gratitude equals great danger. Many times, people in ministry have a superiority complex. We can easily think of ourselves as doing something great for others. This is the opposite of how Jesus wants us to live. We are to be servants of everyone—*everyone*. As Jesus said, "Whoever would be great among you must be your servant, and whoever would be first among you must be slave of all" (Mark 10:43–44 ESV). Gratitude puts us in a posture of servanthood toward others.

Missional people plus gratitude equals an overflow of love and goodness. When we come from a place of gratitude to the Lord for his provision and guidance, then we are grateful for others and see them as gifts and opportunities for love to prevail. Gratitude on mission is essential.

Monica and I use the term "gratvangelism," an amalgamation of the words "gratitude" and "evangelism." It means that when we are carrying the good news to others, we must be permeated with gratitude to the Lord for the opportunity to minister. We must also be filled with gratitude toward the people we are ministering to because if they are allowing us to minister to them, then they are being gracious and kind toward us for even allowing us into their lives. In a number of his writings,

Henri Nouwen spoke of the recipient as enabling the giver.[3] It is not possible for a giver to give gifts if no one is willing to receive the gift. (There may be an offer, but until it is received, the gift is not yet a gift; it is just an offer.) The person being "helped" is the one who is enabling and creating the opportunity for the "helper" to help them. This sounds simple, but it is often overlooked. Once we realize this, gratitude should become our natural response.

Savor the Beauty

Gratitude is part of savoring God's beauty as we experience his joy and goodness and acknowledge his gifts. Gratitude is light within our souls. Non-gratitude in all its forms is darkness within the soul.

Hopefully the theme of abundance is evident in this book. So many of these practices challenge our perspective of lack and scarcity; gratitude is a particularly powerful challenge. When we focus on what we are grateful for, we acknowledge we are not the ones who make them happen. We accept our dependence on God and his goodness, and we are reminded he is good and abundant to us in all aspects of our lives. This practice requires us to have humility and to look to who God is, rather than our own resources.

Practice

Monica and I have mentioned Psalm 103 a few times throughout this book as it reminds us to "forget not all [the Lord's] benefits" (verse 2).

Make a list of his benefits, or blessings, and see how many you can note. You could then write out a prayer or psalm of gratitude in response to this list. Monitor your experience and see how gratitude uplifts your entire day.

After you have experienced this practice, consider how gratitude could become part of your regular times of prayer. Perhaps you could extend your "grace" at mealtimes to include space to share more over your meal. You could include thanksgiving in your journaling practice by writing lists of gratitude every day or each time you journal. You may find them a source of encouragement when you are struggling to feel grateful at other times.

---

3   See Henri J. M. Nouwen, *A Spirituality of Fundraising and A Spirituality of Caregiving* (Upper Room Books, 2010).

Key Resources

- Psalm 136:1–2.

- Philippians 4:6.

- 1 Thessalonians 5:16–18.

- Gary Chapman and Paul White, *The Five Languages of Appreciation in the Workplace: Empowering Organizations by Encouraging People* (Northfield Publishing, 2012). Although this is about gratitude toward others, it also serves as a reminder of how we can be grateful to the Lord.

- Dr. Robert A. Emmons has written several resources on gratitude. He looks specifically at the effects of gratitude on the brain and other areas of life from a psychological perspective. See *Gratitude Works!: A 21-Day Program for Creating Emotional Prosperity* (Jossey-Bass, 2013); (coauthored with Joanne Hill) *The Little Book of Gratitude: Create a Life of Happiness and Wellbeing by Giving Thanks* (Gaia, 2016); *Words of Gratitude: For Mind, Body, and Soul* (Templeton Press, 2020); *Thanks!: How Practicing Gratitude Can Make You Happier* (HarperOne, 2023).

- James Bryan Smith, *The Good and Beautiful God: Falling in Love with the God Jesus Knows* (IVP, 2009). This book tackles the obstacles toward gratitude and opens the reader up to deeper gratitude.

- Ann Voskamp, *One Thousand Gifts: A Dare to Live Fully Right Where You Are* (Thomas Nelson, 2021).

Immersion in Ecclesiastes

Purpose

To get a powerful perspective on life. To experience the growth of our soul and the strengthening of our mind.

Go Deeper

Ecclesiastes is one of the least understood books of wisdom in the Bible, yet because it offers wisdom for the entirety of life, it is also one of the most powerful. Each of the sixty-six books of the Bible has different authorial intentions; the writer of Ecclesiastes aimed to shepherd the hearts and minds of his readers by guiding them through the futility of a godless life to conclude that we can overwhelmingly delight in a good life if we walk with the Lord. I (Jeremy) have done a deeper study through Ecclesiastes each year for the past twenty years. But I also do a quick read-through of it quarterly and *at every major life decision.* Whenever I can't figure out what to do, I read Ecclesiastes, and the power of its wise perspective brings me back to a place of faith and trust in God so I can discern the best path forward. Sometimes Ecclesiastes can be perceived as a negative book … but don't worry, its full force is not pessimistic at all, and when properly understood it is extremely optimistic!

Missional Spirituality

Within Ecclesiastes, the implications for mission are freeing and empowering. The messages bring us into a true perspective of our world, enabling us to see and remove anything that doesn't align with the Lord and allowing us to refocus on the most important and foundational value: knowing God and delighting in him. If we have a foundation of true awe for God, then our values, methodologies, and focus will all fall in line. When we observe his ways and align with him, our love and mission to serve people will be free from codependency, guilt, or false narratives. When we go out on mission in our world, we often see injustice; and it's easy for us to become cynical, doubting that God loves people. Ecclesiastes wrestles with the tensions of injustice and suffering while pointing us to our Creator who wants to cultivate intimacy with his world.

Savor the Beauty

Ecclesiastes draws the attentive reader into the reality that there has never been a more perfect love than God's love, nor a wiser plan than his plan. This book leaves us with a tension of the mysteries beyond our ability to fully understand, and it confronts us with our humanity in the face of God's transcendence. It entices the reader to consider what is preventing them from seeing God's goodness and beauty. Perhaps no other book in the Bible so powerfully recommends the embracing of beauty as much as Ecclesiastes. The author is telling us, "You can enjoy life. You can enjoy life. *You can enjoy life*. And you can do this fully as unto the Lord."

Practice

Read the entire book of Ecclesiastes in one sitting. This isn't meticulous study; this is immersion and encounter. You can read or listen to the book. In audio format it takes about thirty to forty minutes (depending on the version). As you read or listen, consider the entire flow and overarching themes. You may even want to read or listen through it once in the morning and once before bed if you have extra time. Don't try to study or be tedious in your approach. Instead, simply allow the full force of the book to impact you.

As you read, notice where there are positive tones, and how these affirmations regarding life can help you construct an optimistic and well-balanced framework for understanding and living life well. Ask yourself a few helpful questions: What are the major themes? What type of life (and what type of relationship with the Lord) would an author have in order to write a book like this? Does anything upset you, or do you feel resistance to any parts of it? (If so, this is worth prayerfully exploring a bit further.) What might be causing your resistance, and how may the Lord want to speak to you in this?

After you have experienced this practice, consider how you could use Ecclesiastes as part of your decision-making processes. How might you glean more wisdom and understanding from it as a text?

Key Resources

- Ecclesiastes (of course!).

- Jacques Ellul, *Reason for Being: A Meditation on Ecclesiastes* (Eerdmans, 1990). A fascinating and deep reflection on Ecclesiastes. This French philosopher typically did not write on topics like this, but near the end of his life, he wrote a book reflecting on Ecclesiastes and how it was the most significant book throughout his entire life.

- David Gibson, *Living Life Backward: How Ecclesiastes Teaches Us to Live in Light of the End* (Crossway, 2017).

- Douglas Wilson, *Joy at the End of the Tether: The Inscrutable Wisdom of Ecclesiastes* (Canon Press, 1999).

Modified Examen

Purpose

To become more aware of what's happening in our spiritual life and cultivate the practice of honesty before the Lord.

Go Deeper

The practice of Examen involves reflecting on all aspects of our lives, with an openness to God searching our hearts and bringing his wisdom.[1] In the process of discipleship, a maturing follower of Jesus learns to have an interactive relationship with the Father, Son, and Holy Spirit. This is an essential and foundational element of being a disciple. We need to learn from Jesus as our Teacher, following in his words, works, and ways and allowing his worldview, motives, and perspectives to guide how we live. A prayerful examination of our life is a simple way to reorient ourselves away from the default pattern of spiritual self-governance

---

1   We use this term with reference to the Ignatian Examen. Protestant or evangelical readers may feel wary of this because it is rooted in the Catholic tradition. Although we have adapted this from Ignatius of Loyola's "Examen" practice of reflecting on one's outer and inner life and character, we are not aiming for a pure Ignatian approach. Rather, we are aiming to apply the principle of reflection and thoughtfulness. The Scriptures have a lot to say to support this approach to prayer. We use Psalms 42–43 and 139 as a foundational basis. The entire book of Psalms is loaded with examples of self-examination, as is the book of Nehemiah.

toward patterns of humility, where we ask the Lord to show us what he wants. Psalm 139 is a key passage for self-examination before God.

Each element of the process we recommend for this practice is scripturally based. We are invited to begin our prayer time with rejoicing and thanksgiving. We then let our requests be made known to God. We take inventory of what he is doing in and around us (learning to be attentive to the King and his kingdom). We turn away from false idols and attitudes, and we return to the call he has placed on each of us. Finally, we reorient ourselves toward the direction he is leading us in, with an ear to his Spirit.

This practice has been transformative for me (Monica). For a long time I had practiced being in God's presence regularly, but when I started practicing the Examen daily, it allowed me to notice more of what God was doing and how he was ministering to me in small moments throughout my day. It's so easy to function on autopilot, and this practice revealed how often I don't pay attention to what he might be doing. Over time, I was able to gain a greater awareness of God moving and speaking. This gave me the clarity I needed to make some tough decisions. I also consciously acknowledged to God the things I often left under the surface without dealing with them.

Missional Spirituality

Sadly, the evidence of those who are not engaging in spiritual reflection is easy to see. The seemingly unceasing tide of ministry corruption and moral failures from those engaging in God's mission seems to point to a lack of attention toward our inner lives. Without this practice of self-examination, we fail ourselves and others, undermining the kingdom work we have been part of. Incorporating regular patterns of recollection and reflection enables us to have "Eyes in our heads" (Eccles. 2:14). As Desert Mother Amma Syncletica said,

> *A [person] whose house is about to fall down may invite travelers inside to refresh them, but instead they will be hurt in the collapse of the house. It is the same with teachers who have not carefully trained themselves in the good life;*[2] *they destroy their hearers as well*

---

2   By "good life" she is referring to a life that is imbued with the goodness of the Lord and his kingdom.

as themselves. Their mouth invites to salvation, their way of life leads to ruin.[3]

If we are to embody Jesus to those around us, we cannot sidestep this important process of bringing our whole selves to the Lord and allowing him to form us more deeply.

Savor the Beauty

This practice makes us aware of the tangents God leads us on, so that we may appreciate the scenic view. We often drift through life with no thought toward reflection or personal awareness of what is really happening around, in, or to us. But engaging with the Examen aids our ability to remember the good things the Lord has done, as well as remember our frailty and his mercy. In practicing the Examen, we find ourselves reminded that God's mercy endures forever. Jeremy and I have found this practice builds our sense of humility and respect before the Lord, as well as our awareness that he is always with us. We have also noticed it helps us extend more grace to others around us! In the careful inspection that comes from the Examen, we are reminded that all need grace from the Lord and that we can be conduits of grace toward others in our lives.

Practice

The Examen is the process of taking a personal inventory from the day and praying through the process (or, if you're doing this in the morning, you can think about your day yesterday). You may want to journal this. You could use this helpful outline:

- *Rejoice*: List some things you can rejoice over and be thankful for.

- *Request*: Ask the Lord to show you any area he wants to be at work within you and where he was speaking and moving throughout your day.

---

3 Amma Syncletica, quoted in *The Sayings of the Desert Fathers: The Alphabetical Collection*, Benedicta Ward (Translator) (Liturgical Press, 1975), Saying 74, 105. You can find more of her quotes and others of the early church fathers and mothers in *The Sayings of the Desert Fathers* and Benedicta Ward, ed., *The Desert Fathers: Sayings of the Early Christian Monks* (Penguin, 2003).

- *Review*: Reflect on God's presence in your life today. What has he been doing? Where and when did you notice him? Did he give you any invitations or promptings? How did you respond to his promptings and voice?

- *Repent*: Ask him where you need to see change in your life. Are there things he is calling you to turn away from? Are there other things he is inviting you into?

- *Renew*: Focus forward on where he is calling you in the coming day, week, month, and year. Where do you desire his work to become more evident?

After you have experienced this practice, consider whether there is there a natural time in your schedule when you have space to practice this more regularly. You may also find the benefits of practicing the Examen at seasonal intervals, perhaps as part of a quarterly retreat or your annual planning.

Key Resources

- Philippians 1:9–11.

- Colossians 1:9–11.

- Adele Ahlberg Calhoun, *Spiritual Disciplines Handbook: Practices That Transform Us* (IVP, 2015). See section on Examen.

- Ignatius of Loyola, *The Spiritual Exercises of Saint Ignatius: Saint Ignatius' Profound Precepts of Mystical Theology*, Anthony Mottola (Translator) (Doubleday Publishing Group, 1964).

Three Readings

Purpose

To move beyond mere analysis of the Word toward a deeper, transformative, and prayerful encounter with the Lord through Scripture.

Go Deeper

This practice involves reading a short passage of the Bible three times. In church history, this is referred to as *lectio divina* (divine reading).

It has a mind-oriented part (*lectio*), which is a prayerful reading; a heart-oriented part (*meditatio*), which is a reflective consideration of what the Lord highlights to you in the passage; and a soul-oriented part (*contemplatio*), which is an experiential embracing of the truths the Lord is presenting to you.

We can often come to Scripture with a more analytic focus, ready to dissect the passage. With this practice we are aiming to meditate on a passage long enough to allow God to speak to us through it and for it to change us. We listen to what the Lord highlights to us and ask what he wants us to pay attention to and potentially act upon.

This practice can also help us remember God's Word. Multiple readings of a passage make it more familiar, and we may find we have almost memorized it by the time we have finished. However, the goal isn't simply rote learning but instead to spend time abiding in the Lord through his Word, without rushing or trying to get anything specific out of it. We surrender our agendas when we come to Scripture and allow God to be the One who uses the time in his way. This practice is less about getting information and more about meeting with God. It should be a conversation with him. Here are some passages we suggest starting with, but you could use any shorter portion of Scripture to do this: Matthew 11:25–30, 1 Corinthians 13, and Colossians 1:15–20.

Missional Spirituality

When we are on mission, we often have a "get things done" or "make things happen" approach. We can even get into that habit when we interact with God himself. But when we give space for God to speak to us through his Word and submit to this practice, we confront our temptation to be in control. Our aim on mission is to invite others into the beautiful kingdom of our God. When we practice *lectio divina*, we place ourselves in a posture of receiving from God and experiencing his kingdom at a deeper level. We will then be more equipped and strengthened to give to and receive from others.

Savor the Beauty

This practice is about *really* savoring. When we are told to meditate on the Word "day and night" (Ps. 1:2) we are encouraged to keep reflecting and unpacking the goodness and richness of the Bible. Scripture is breathed by God (2 Tim. 3:16), so why wouldn't it be something of mind-boggling depth? Reading a passage once through is a good practice that allows us to grasp a bit more of God. And to read it a second time is to step a bit deeper into our relationship with him. We have an opportunity to further grow in our understanding of who God is and how we relate to him. It is intimate. We pay attention to whatever it is that he may have for us within the text. We listen to what he wants to say to us. But the third reading is the point where we have the opportunity for our heart and soul to no longer simply look for information and understanding; instead, we receive his power and love. It allows the Holy Spirit to speak to us in a deeply transformative way. This is intended to bring us out of cursory or obligatory readings of Scripture and into the life-changing richness where Jesus wants to meet us.

Practice

Pick a short passage. Read it once and reflect upon it. What is highlighted to you? It may be just one word. Take one or two minutes of silence before reading it a second time more prayerfully, with a special focus on the highlighted portion. Take another one or two minutes of silence before reading it a third time. On this third reading, take more time to focus on the highlighted section. As you read the words, wait for a few moments, and ask God to open your eyes and reveal to you the wondrous things from his Word (Ps. 119:18). Talk to him about what you believe he is saying, and then spend some more time in silence in his presence.

After you have experienced this practice, consider how you could make time to do repeated readings of the Bible passages you read as part of your regular devotional time.

Key Resources

- Deuteronomy 30:14.

- Psalms 1; 19; 119.

- Hebrews 4:12–13.

- Adele Ahlberg Calhoun, *Spiritual Disciplines Handbook: Practices That Transform Us* (IVP, 2015). See section on Lectio Divina and Devotional Reading.

- Richard J. Foster, *Celebration of Discipline: The Path to Spiritual Growth* (Hodder & Stoughton, 2008).

- Dallas Willard, *The Spirit of the Disciplines: Understanding How God Changes Lives* (Harper, 2002) and *Renovation of the Heart: Putting on the Character of Christ*, 20th anniversary edition (NavPress, 2021).

Prayer of Recollection

Purpose

To bring all the areas of our inward and outward beings before the Lord, choosing to give these to him so we aren't trying to carry them alone. To move away from worry and toward peace, grace, and love from God, knowing we can cast our cares upon him because he cares for us (1 Pet. 5:7).

Go Deeper

Sometimes we struggle to pray because we feel distracted by our to-do lists and other concerns. We can even feel shame and guilt about our imperfections, which may stop us from coming to God. The prayer of recollection is the practice of being honest with God, who is not surprised at our weaknesses and who looks on us with love and a longing to connect. This practice can help us break out of worry or a perfectionist mentality and allow us to be like children who can bring their wants, needs, and cares to their good Father. This may initially require great courage, as we may fear God's disappointment. But remember that each of us is beloved. God wants us to come to him exactly as we are, with all our requests (Phil. 4:6), and to experience his perfect love that casts out fear (1 John 4:18).

This practice cultivates a keen sense of awareness: we become more aware of the things disturbing us, but then we become aware of God's supernatural power to bring resolve, peace, completeness, and wholeness to those disparate struggles. Being attentive helps us to be prepared to respond to God in all things. Peace may not be immediately accessible with this practice, but that's fine; that is the point of practicing! We are training ourselves to be more open toward God ministering to our hearts, minds, and souls.

Many of the psalms are practices of recollection: the psalmists often lift their cares to the Lord in total honesty, exposing their weaknesses and pleading for grace. A typical pattern found in the psalms is a movement away from disorientation toward recollection and peace in the face of great trials. If you are facing troubles, take note of Psalms 42–43 where the psalmist asks *his own soul* why he is downcast. This is a moment of opportunity for the psalmist to experience recollection. He then *tells his own soul* to trust in God. How often have you tried talking to your own soul, or telling your own soul to trust in the Lord?

Missional Spirituality

In mission work there are many ways to be peacemakers, but if our interior condition isn't at peace with the Lord, we are often unable to bring peace to those around us. If we practice recollection, we will build a muscle of abiding in peace consistently, even while we are involved in our work. This practice has helped Jeremy and I to shift back into a state of peacefulness, even in moments of chaos.

Many times we can experience "mission drift" where we lose focus and direction in the midst of the work God has called us to. A prayer of recollection allows us to return to the Lord and refocus our priorities, remembering where we get our peace and surety from. When we are rooted in God's peace, we are better able to emanate his presence in our missional context.

Savor the Beauty

Based on the principles from Philippians 4, we can trade our worries for peace:

The Lord is near. Do not worry about anything, but in everything by prayer and supplication with thanksgiving let your requests be made known to God. And the peace of God, which surpasses all understanding, will guard your hearts and your minds in Christ Jesus.

Finally, beloved, whatever is true, whatever is honorable, whatever is just, whatever is pure, whatever is pleasing, whatever is commendable, if there is any excellence, and if there is anything worthy of praise, think about these things. Keep on doing the things that you have learned and received and heard and seen in me, and the God of peace will be with you.

PHILIPPIANS 4:5–9 NRSV

What beautiful freedom we are invited to here! We are not told to ignore the things troubling us but instead to share them with God. We are told here to "keep on doing" the things Paul practiced (verse 9). The Philippians had an advantage, as they received, saw, and heard these things first-hand, but we also have an advantage as we have the fullness of Scripture that reveals to us a great number of practices we can imitate, not just from Paul but from many people of faith. That's what these thirty-one days are all about—putting into practice the things that focus our attention on Christ and foster growth in our faith.

Practice

Begin your time of reflection by taking some deep breaths and quieting your body. As stray thoughts or worries come into your mind, lift them individually to the Lord and ask him to bring you back to a place of peace. Sometimes, Jeremy and I have found it helpful to physically lift our hands as we do this. It may also help to write each concern on a small piece of paper, fold it up, and place it in a jar as a symbolic representation of releasing it to God. At the end, you can throw them all away as another act of trusting God with your cares. Keep giving over every thought to him and try to stay in a place of prayer until you have connected with the peace of God, even if this takes a bit more time than anticipated.

After you have experienced this practice, consider how you may incorporate this practice as part of your other times of prayer. It can be easy to bring a rushed list of requests to God in prayer without a sense of releasing those worries or waiting for his peace to come. You may find journaling some of your thoughts during this time (even as a bullet-point list) could help you to give these things over to God. When engaged in times of prayer with others, how may you lead them in this practice to help them receive more of God's peace?

Key Resources

- Psalms 116:7; 131:2.

- Matthew 11:28.

- Ephesians 3:14–21.

- Adele Ahlberg Calhoun, "Prayer of Recollection," in *Spiritual Disciplines Handbook: Practices That Transform Us* (IVP, 2015), 281.

- Richard J. Foster, *Prayer: Finding the Heart's True Home* (HarperOne, 2002). See section on "prayer of recollection."

- Saint Teresa of Avila, *The Interior Castle* (Tan Books, 2011). Specifically the 4th Dwelling.

Listening to Others

Purpose

To learn to listen and subsequently learn to love more deeply with a posture of true humility toward others.

Go Deeper

This is one of the simplest but most unapplied spiritual practices. Many of society's problems stem from an inability to listen to others. Picture the transformation that could occur if there was a revolution of people who went out and listened to people with intentions of love. What if we began to think of others more highly than ourselves (as we are commanded to do in Philippians 2:3)? What if we humbled ourselves and interacted with others with a demeanor of love? What if we asked the Lord to show us the image of God in those around us? In his famous essay, "The Weight of Glory," C. S. Lewis notes we can't fully fathom the glorious beauty God has put in other humans.[1] If we could see this beauty in others, it would change how we live.

---

1   C. S. Lewis, *The Weight of Glory: And Other Addresses: No. 15*, New ed. (HarperOne, 2001).

Whereas talking can be used as a means to dominate, control, or manipulate others, listening can empower the one being listened to, as well as transform the listener themselves. Instead of talking to project our own image into the world, when we train ourselves to listen, we surrender our image and reputation. We become less worried about what others think of us and experience the freedom of truly seeing and listening to those in our midst.

We also exercise true humility as we begin listening to others' experiences. We are drawn toward the genuine celebration of others and increase what Timothy Keller refers to as "self-forgetfulness."[2] We become ready to care, ready to demonstrate kindness, and ready to love. By listening to others, we experience the beauty of self-control as a good and enjoyable fruit of the Spirit, instead of viewing it as a self-imposed loss. The art of listening trains our hearts toward gentleness and enables love to exude from our presence toward those around us.

 ## Missional Spirituality

People are suffering all around us, though some hide it better than others. To be heard is to be served. By listening, we give others dignity, respect, and honor. We allow them space to process what's happening in their lives and to be cared for by others (whether by simply being listened to or through practical action). We create opportunities to build trust, and we ask the Holy Spirit to bring replenishment to the person sharing as we have these conversations.

Listening to others doesn't mean we don't get to talk or respond. On the contrary, listening well allows us to know when we should respond in a way that will bless the other. It also adds gravitas to our words later when the time to speak arises. Most people don't want to hear someone's thoughts or advice until they know the other person cares for them. We are in danger of putting the cart before the horse if we try to convince others to listen to us before showing we love them enough to listen to them.

Listening is a form of hospitality that cannot be ignored by those who aim to be on mission with Jesus. In listening to others, we offer them welcome and a place to share and be heard. Listening also helps us to discern what the Lord is doing in their lives. This means listening is an active, participatory practice. Too often, people assume if they're not talking, then they're not participating—but this isn't true. As we

---

2   See Timothy Keller, *The Freedom of Self Forgetfulness: The Path to True Christian Joy* (10Publishing, 2012).

listen attentively to the person (and to God), we fully participate in holding a sacred space for the speaker. In *The Contemplative Pastor*, Eugene Peterson highlights the value of listening for the conversation the Lord is already having with a person before speaking into the conversation as well.[3] This attitude encourages us to reflect: *God is at work here in this person in front of me; I shouldn't butt into the conversation until I understand what is happening and can speak with wisdom.* A helpful rhythm is that of "watch, wait, walk." We *watch* to see what the Lord is doing, *wait* until the time is ready, then *walk* with him into where he is leading. This requires listening.

Savor the Beauty

If we learn to listen to others, we will find that God reveals his image in them to us. In listening, we also get a greater sense of God's heart of love toward the person speaking and an insight into the things he is doing in and through their lives (whether they know it or not). This practice builds our faith and trust because we see God at work and notice his movements.

Practice

Make it your aim today to speak less, listen more, and ask good questions. If there is someone you know who needs to be heard, seek them out and give them time to share. Try asking an open-ended question and then leave space to hear their full response. While you are listening, ask what God may be doing in the other person's life and that he would reveal himself to you through them. Be open to learning from this person through what they share, but also be ready to show love, encouragement, and support.

After you have experienced this practice, consider if there is a person or a context where you could listen to others more regularly. Is there someone in your life to whom you could give time on a daily or weekly basis, making space for them to share and for you to listen to them? What are some of the areas where you need to improve your listening skills, and how could you go about learning to do this better? Are there ways you need to practice listening well in your Christian community? How can you encourage a culture of good listening?

---

3   See Eugene Peterson, *The Contemplative Pastor: Returning to the Art of Spiritual Direction* (Eerdmans, 1993), 60.

Key Resources

- 1 Samuel 3:10.

- Romans 12:3.

- Philippians 2:3.

- Renovaré's "Fellowship of the Burning Heart" groups, https://renovare.org/burningheart. Renovaré offers excellent listening groups for training people to listen to each other and the Spirit. We have been participating in these for a while and have experienced personal and ministerial transformation through these groups.

- Jeremy and Monica Chambers, *Kingdom Contours: Empowering Everyday People With the Tools to Shape Kingdom Movements* (Missional Challenge, 2020). Throughout chapter three, we address the importance of missional practitioners learning to listen. We also note that this is vital for contextualization as a missionary who is attentive to the needs of those around them.

- Duane Elmer, *Cross-Cultural Servanthood: Serving the World in Christlike Humility* (IVP, 2006). This book is incredibly sensitive toward loving others in the ways they need to be loved with insight toward being a listener.

- Hugh Halter and Matt Smay, *The Tangible Kingdom Primer* (Missio Publishing, 2009). This has an excellent section on gospel listening.

- Dallas Willard, *Hearing God: Developing a Conversational Relationship with God* (IVP, 2012). This is primarily a text on being attentive to God, but the insights are transferable.

Breath Prayer
and Centering Prayer

Purpose

To discover how easily and quickly we can come directly before the throne of God to receive mercy and help in times of need (Heb. 4:16).

Go Deeper

Breath prayers and centering prayers assist us in refocusing our attention on God through a brief moment using simple words. We can do this intermittently throughout our day or for longer periods. Although words are involved in these prayers, there is a relinquishing of "wordiness" in order to learn how to go beyond our words in communion with God.

As we repeat particular words or phrases, we allow them to have a deeper spiritual impact on our lives. For example, when praying the word "peace" throughout the day, peace itself may seem to gain power in our lives. As a child, I (Jeremy) often prayed for peace, but I hadn't yet experienced the supernatural peace of God. As I encountered genuine peace and recognized God's increasing redemptive work in every area of my life, the word "peace" had a powerful impact on my heart, soul, mind, and spirit. Jesus' assurance has become even more meaningful for me when he says, "Peace I leave with you; my peace I give to you. Not as the world gives do I give to you" (John 14:27 ESV). So the more I repeat this word and experience its depths, the more the peace Jesus gives becomes distinguished to me from the alleged peace the world offers.

Missional Spirituality

Living missionally can be stressful, especially if we are not recentering on the King of the mission. The trials and dangers we face can seem daunting. But returning to God regularly in prayer changes everything. This practice is a great way to carry a request throughout our day or to remind ourselves of the perspective we need. It helps us to meditate on the Lord in all aspects of our work and mission. Through prayers like this, we can reimagine our mission in light of the overflow of his constant presence, and we can experience mission as a partnership, with Jesus right beside us every step of the way.

Savor the Beauty

This practice can allow us to contemplate and experience new aspects of who God is. We can savor the unchangeableness of God, his faithfulness, his active shepherding presence in our lives, and the fact that he walks beside us, dwells in us, and holds us in every circumstance we face. This gives us a prolonged meditation upon God's character and fruit that could yield something deep in our life.

Practice

These are two separate practices that are based on similar foundations. You can try both or pick one for the day.

Breath prayer is a simple prayer small enough to be prayed in one breath. Some people pick a name of God and pray it as they breathe in and out. Others may take a small request and pray it over and over. This is not the vain repetition Jesus warns against (Matt. 6:7); instead it is a continual yielding to his sovereignty and a worshipful embracing of who he is. Some breathe in a name of God while breathing out a brief request or statement of truth, for example: "Father, I am Yours," or "Lord of Armies, protect me," or "Provider, please provide!" or "Comforter, I need your comfort."

Centering prayer is similar, but perhaps simpler, as it usually focuses on just one word. You can try picking a fruit of the Spirit or a name of God and returning to it throughout the day. But when you return to this word as a prayer, lift it to the Lord as a request, as worship, as receptivity, and as realization altogether. For example, on a day when you may be facing some difficulties, you can choose "peace" as your word of centering prayer. You can pray this constantly as a request for peace, or as a proclamation that you choose his peace, or as a realization that Jesus is the Prince of Peace.

You may want to use these prayers in a dispersed way throughout your day by returning to the practice multiple times for just a few seconds or minutes. Or you may want to use these prayers for several specific times that are longer, such as morning, noon, and night. For a longer session, try setting a timer for ten minutes and begin by stilling yourself and being silent before the Lord as you allow your whole mind and being to focus on him. You may want to light a candle to help you focus. Take a deep breath, remember his presence, and use the breath prayer or centering prayer to bring your wandering thoughts back to him. Repeat this process for the whole time.

After you have experienced this practice, consider if there are particular words for centering prayer that you could use more regularly, to help you when you are facing particular situations. Perhaps you could write some breath prayers to return to at certain times, such as before a difficult meeting or task, or before spending time with a person you are struggling with.

Key Resources

- Psalm 62:1.

- Luke 1:46.

- 2 Peter 1:3–4.

- Revelation 4.

- Adele Ahlberg Calhoun, *Spiritual Disciplines Handbook: Practices That Transform Us* (IVP, 2015). See sections on breath prayer and centering prayer.

- Richard J. Foster, *Longing for God: Seven Paths of Christian Devotion* (IVP, 2016). See "Pathway Six: Action and Contemplation." Foster uses the example of John Cassian, "Balancing the Active and Contemplative Life" (p. 205), which we consider vital for the missional practitioner who aims to embody the values of centering prayer. Foster's other example of "Gregory the Great: Living the Active Life Contemplatively" is an excellent example of how to balance these values.

Secrecy

Purpose

To experience the beauty and joy of humility and to discover that doing good for the sake of the Lord, without praise from others, is truly enjoyable.

Go Deeper

Oh how duplicitous our hearts can be! How double-minded and double-intentioned we can be. Our hearts can be deceptive to the point that we even do acts of kindness with poor motives. But God has called us to be holy (1 Pet. 1:15–16), and to live lives like Jesus, serving sacrificially and not seeking to manage our reputations. In today's culture there is an assumption that unless we show people what we did, it didn't happen. But as we learn in Matthew 6, God sees what is done in secret, and he is the only one we should focus on. In this passage Jesus preached on three activities that should be done in secret: giving to the needy, prayer, and fasting. Rather than indulging in our fleeting desire to be seen, Jesus invites us to lay up treasures in heaven, where our hearts must be, and to not be anxious. When we trust that God sees what is done in secret, we know he also sees what we need. If we live in light of Matthew 6, then when we practice righteous secrecy, we remind ourselves this world is not our home, and we are not meant to receive things from this world that can only be received in his kingdom.

When we begin to practice this, many of us will begin to realize how much we are motivated by a desire for recognition. However, the more we practice it, the more we can eventually feel the freedom to automatically do anonymous acts of good. We will no longer need to be seen and can instead enjoy the goodness done in quiet. This will also overflow into other areas of our lives. For example, it may help us to keep things confidential for the sake of protecting the reputations of others and to care more about honoring and giving dignity to others.

It's good to strategize about an act of goodness you can do without receiving any recognition. The enemy strategizes all the time about evil. Proverbs tells us often about the feet of the wicked who run quickly to evil schemes (6:18). The inverse is true of the righteous: the righteous person schemes about how to do beautiful and good things for others.

Missional Spirituality

There are good deeds that need to be seen in order to give glory to the Father—Jesus tells us so in Matthew 5:16. However, it is beneficial to train ourselves while on mission to have the humility to *not* be seen from time to time. Jeremy and I have friends who critique Christianity because they perceive that some Christians are seeking recognition on social media for their ministry achievements or want to be seen as super-righteous people. Our non-believing friends see these people as self-absorbed because of this. Small, hidden acts can therefore be more powerful.

To be on mission is to be a witness—a testimony to the integrity of the message and hope of Jesus Christ. Jesus himself was willing to do much that we don't know about, as John tells us: "The whole world does not have room for the books that would be written" (John 21:25). And throughout the Gospels, we see Jesus often asked people to keep silent about his good deeds. Jesus was also prepared to be rejected, despised, and crucified rather than seek the glory and reputation he deserved. We may often feel the need to look good or prove we are ministering or achieving something in our work. But to minister quietly and secretly and go unnoticed is a means of purifying our missional activity in such a way we echo John the Baptist's words, "He must increase, but I must decrease" (John 3:30 ESV).

Savor the Beauty

To let God increase and allow ourselves to decrease in the minds of others is an aim worth practicing. Again, to use Timothy Keller's term, we become "self-forgetful" in this practice.[1] The glory of God, and the beauty of him receiving praise and adoration, becomes something that drives us. We believe our eyes are best opened to his glory when we are not consumed with a selfish gaze. His beauty will shine clearer to the one who is most concerned with promoting and enjoying his beauty in this world.

Practice

Do something good for someone. Do it without anyone ever knowing. Earlier in the month you practiced acts of kindness and generosity (see pages 69–72), but this time you are training yourself to do good even when no one notices. If this practice dents your pride, take some time to pray and process your feelings and thoughts with God. How may he want to encourage you to receive affirmation from him rather than those around you?

After you have experienced this practice, consider how you could more regularly seek to give glory to God rather than yourself.

---

1 See Timothy Keller, *The Freedom of Self Forgetfulness: The Path to True Christian Joy* (10Publishing, 2012).

Key Resources

- Matthew 6.

- Mark 7:36 (reflect on the context).

- John 3:30.

- Adele Ahlberg Calhoun, *Spiritual Disciplines Handbook: Practices That Transform Us* (IVP, 2015). See section on secrecy.

- Sara Hagerty, *Unseen: The Gift of Being Hidden in a World That Loves To Be Noticed* (Zondervan, 2017).

Missional Sentness

Purpose

To reconnect with our vision and calling, recalling how the Lord has led us to where we are now and how he's sent us out into his harvest—and to discover where he may be sending us next.[1]

Go Deeper

We can often be in danger of setting up a false dichotomy between "intimacy" with the Father and "mission." But there is no true mission without intimacy with the Father, and there is no true intimacy with the Father unless we are willing to follow him into the mission he has prepared for us. If Jesus is drawing us into a deeper walk with him, then his call to "follow me … and I will send you out to fish for people" (Matt. 4:19) is also a call for us. That's what the art of missional spirituality is all about. Having been involved in missionary work our whole lives, Monica and I are saddened by the reality that many missions focus on going in "Jesus' name" without investing in the importance of having Jesus

---

1   See also appendix 2 on "A Weekly Rhythm" for a deeper look at how we may embrace mission weekly.

along with us, or really knowing Jesus as we go.[2] As missional disciples, we must first receive his love, and then we love others because he first loved us (1 John 4:19). Just as the disciples spent time with Jesus, we need to know who he is and his voice, otherwise we may get off-course from his mission.

We can't skip mission and just pursue the intimacy part either! God is a missionary God. He sent his Son as the quintessential missionary, and the Son has sent us. Throughout church history, there have been many ascetics who withdrew into solitude for a season, but all who were effective still had care and concern for others. Spiritual formation is inextricably linked with caring for those around us, all of whom are image-bearers of God. There is no spiritual formation in permanent isolation. In his helpful resource *Longing for God,* Richard Foster maps out seven historic paths or approaches to intimacy with God.[3] One of those paths is titled "Action and Contemplation," where Foster explores the lives of John Cassian, Benedict of Nursia, and Gregory the Great. Each of these men was known for recognizing the need for deep intimacy with Christ while never giving up on the vitality of mission. They saw a way to straddle the tension between service to God and creating space to withdraw periodically to foster intimacy with God. In our first book *Kingdom Contours,* Monica and I refer to this as "semi-monastic," or being able to withdraw for a time before coming back for mission.[4] We also explain what we call "strategic spirituality," which is a missionally-oriented form of action and contemplation where we unpack this idea of intimacy with God while on mission with him.[5]

Missional Spirituality

Many in ministry leadership are spiritually unhealthy—doing great deeds on the outside but full of deadness on the inside, just as Jesus spoke so clearly of the Pharisees in Matthew 23. But this would not be the case if we valued the integrity of intimacy with the Lord as *a key part of* our missional sentness.

2   As our friend Tyler Yoder pointed out, in Matthew 16, Peter got the mission confused, and Jesus rebuked him, calling him back to set his mind on the things of God rather than the things of people.

3   This is not to be confused with Foster's other book, *Streams of Living Water,* which focuses on six "streams" within historic Christianity. Rather, *Longing for God* looks more specifically at seven approaches to devotion toward the Lord. Richard Foster, *Longing for God: Seven Paths of Christian Devotion,* Reprint ed. (IVP, 2016).

4   Chambers, *Kingdom Contours: Empowering Everyday People With the Tools to Shape Kingdom Movements* (Missional Challenge, 2020), 26.

5   Ibid., 54–56.

When we find intimacy with God, he redirects our mission and gives us a greater sense of who we are called to be, as well as where and to whom we are called. Because he truly knows us, we can be sure he will send us into something that matches our personality and skills—and we can trust him even when we feel stretched beyond our comfort zone. When we operate from a place of intimacy, we are motivated by love rather than guilt or a sense that we "should" be on mission. Our mission pours out of the overflow of our life with him.

Savor the Beauty

Without Jesus, there is no true beauty to be found while on mission. But when we partner and spend time with Jesus as we are on mission, we will find his beauty to be everywhere.

In 2008, I (Jeremy) went with some friends to share the good news with students at a college in Chicago. Just before we left, one of the fellow students, whose prayer life and missional fervency I greatly admired, prayed, "God, you are so beautiful." He said it with such conviction that it struck me in a way I had never thought of before: God is beautiful! Why hadn't I ever really thought about this? Afterward, I kept thinking of the beauty of God, seeing his beauty all around me and in those I spoke with. This changed not only the way I spoke to others but also how I listened to them. When we grow in our intimacy with God and see more of his beauty, it transforms the way we share his goodness with others.

Practice

Take some time to quiet yourself in the Lord's presence. Remember that the Father has you in his hands, the Spirit indwells you and intercedes for you, and Jesus walks with you and calls you "friend." It is in this intimate presence of the Triune God, that you can ask the Lord to speak to you on these following areas.

- *How is Jesus leading you into his mission?* The answer here may flow out of the giftings and vision he has laid on your heart, or perhaps the people or places you sense he has called you to.

- *Who listens to you?* Consider the people whom God has given you grace or favor to speak into their lives. These may be people he has strategically put in your circle of influence.

- *Is there a ministry you haven't experimented with yet?* Perhaps he is calling you into something new and different.

In which of the following five activities do you sense the greatest joy? Your answer may reveal a pathway that the Lord is leading you into. It will also reveal something special about the way the Lord has intimately wired and gifted you to participate in his kingdom work.

- When the body is mobilized to do ministry and take new ground.
- When the body expresses faithfulness and intimacy with the Lord.
- When good news is being shared.
- When people are loving and caring toward one another, *being* the body to one another.
- When teaching is solid and biblically/theologically grounded.

Pray about the topics addressed in this practice and specifically ask the Lord to reveal a pathway forward that honors his mission while drawing you deeper into intimacy with him. Maybe journal with a prayerful question to the Lord, asking, "Where and/ or to whom are you sending me?" This isn't with the assumption that he will call you halfway around the world, but instead that he may call you to cross the street to visit a neighbor or friend.[6]

After you have experienced this practice, consider how God may be inviting you to draw away in intimacy with him more while you are on mission. How may you pursue intimacy with God during your mission?

---

6   Of course, we wouldn't deny that he may send you overseas. But you can be a missionary crossing cultures right where you are.

Key Resources

- Philippians 3:7–14. (This passage perfectly exemplifies missional sentness!)

- Jeremy and Monica Chambers, *Kingdom Contours: Empowering Everyday People With the Tools to Shape Kingdom Movements* (Missional Challenge, 2020). We condense the best points of over a hundred books on missional "sentness" in one place—a foundational starting point for those who are beginning to dig into missional discipleship and lifestyle.

Present Your Body
as a Living Sacrifice

Purpose

To uncover the joy of seeing our bodies as God has made them. To recognize that we are well created and that God chose to give us bodies for a reason, not just because he needed a house for our spirits, but because he valued creating us in the physical realm.

Go Deeper

Romans 12:1 says to, "Present your bodies as a living sacrifice, holy and acceptable to God, which is your spiritual worship" (ESV). We can sometimes feel uncomfortable viewing our bodies as having anything to do with spiritual realities, and we inadvertently create a false sacred/secular divide. Yet God designed our bodies in such a way that they reflect our souls. For example, our faces show inward realities (more than we may want sometimes). Our mouths either spew out curses or flow with thanksgivings and encouragements. Our eyes reflect light or darkness. Our hands care for others or harm them. It seems our bodies are more connected to our spiritual reality than we often think.

When Jesus put on flesh, he communicated goodness about our bodies—he wanted to fully experience and identify with us in our humanness. God wants us to experience his truths and goodness through our bodies, and we won't experience the fullness of his goodness unless our bodies are also involved. God designed and loves our bodies. He longs for us to love them as well, to see them as his intentionally and well-designed creations. When we offer our bodies as living sacrifices, we recognize our bodies are not our own. We are Christ's, and because of that, we offer our bodies as well as the rest of ourselves to him. Too often, we offer him our hearts, our minds, our spirits, and our souls, but we don't think to offer him our bodies. When God asks us to love him with all our strength (Mark 12:30), he is calling us to love him with our bodies, where our strength resides.

I (Jeremy) was about twenty years old when I first engaged with this practice. At that time I felt a lot of guilt and shame in connection with my body and who I was. I had to remind myself there is grace and freedom in Jesus. As I have continued to practice this over the years, I have increasingly been able to look at my body and recognize that God has created me well, and he has allowed my body to be a conduit of love and grace to others. I now understand that through my body I represent Jesus. I bear his image. And so I ask the Lord to take each part of my body and use it for his glory.

Whenever I (Monica) do this exercise, I ask Jesus for every part of my body to mirror his goodness: *May my eyes look at others as yours look at others. May my smile be your smile. May my hands be like your hands. May my arms embrace as yours embrace.* I come back to this prayer and desire often, especially as I prepare to meet and interact with others.

Although the fall produced shame in Adam and Eve's bodies, because of Jesus' redemptive work on the cross we no longer need to feel that way. Though Adam and Eve wanted to cover up, becoming judges of their bodies' goodness or lack of it (Gen. 3:7), we can now receive healing in our bodies in ways that will affect our hearts, souls, and how we relate to others. In this practice, we offer our bodies to God as a living sacrifice. We remove our longing to judge. We receive his perspective of our bodies. This can be a scary and vulnerable practice, but remember you are offering your body to the good and loving God who knitted you together in your mother's womb (Ps. 139:13). He thinks you are incredible! He sees the wonderful creation he has made, even if you may perceive it as marred or scarred. Receive his love for you through your body all the way to the depths of your soul.[1]

---

1 This practice has been known to be simultaneously triggering and yet deeply healing for those who have encountered abuse in their past. We suggest that the reader, "do as you can, not as you can't" with respect to this practice. The goal is to present your body to Jesus and allow him to speak to you concerning how he sees you.

Missional Spirituality

As bearers of good news in the world, we need to remember the good news resides in our very bodies. We can receive his redemptive perspective on how we see our bodies. We can receive his peace and comfort when our bodies are in pain. We can see his goodness working through our bodies as we share with others, whether through speaking, singing, walking, or serving with our hands.

So as you do this practice, allow the good news to permeate your body. Let this be a moment where hope conquers doubt. This will influence how you help others around you. When you see your body as a part of the good work God has done in you, you will feel compelled to share more hope, love, and joy with others. When you see the good news permeates your body, your whole presence will exude Jesus' love and good news in and through you.

Savor the Beauty

Today, savor the good news that God is with you. Savor the truth that he loves you and made you well. Savor the beauty God put in your body. He made you. You don't have the authority to say that your body is not beautifully made. Let's say that again: you do not *ever* have the authority to say that something he made is not beautiful. Please don't ever assume you can neglect this great truth.

Although the effects of the fall have come upon us, and we struggle with all sorts of physical limitations and pain, it is still true that he left his image in us. Whatever damage we may have experienced to our bodies, God never took away his image in us or his love for us. Just as we look at nature and see God's beauty, when we look at ourselves in the mirror, we are looking at his creation. Savor what he has made.

Practice

"Present your bodies as a living sacrifice, holy and acceptable to God, which is your spiritual worship" (Rom. 12:1 ESV). Consider how your body may be offered to the Lord and how he has made you well. You might want to lie on the floor and offer each part of your body from the crown of your head down to your toes, spending time conversing with God about each one and lifting it to him. Or, using a mirror, literally look at various parts of your body and consider how God made them. Offer them up to him for his purposes. Pay attention to what you feel and think as you look at yourself.

If guilt or difficult emotions arise, surrender, repent of whatever you need to turn from, and receive his grace, love, and mercy. You are free in Christ. You are forgiven and loved and fully accepted. If shame arises, bring it before the Lord and consider if there are any lies you believe about your body that he wants to bring truth to. If anger surfaces, take note, and consider whether you need to talk with someone who can help you experience healing and forgiveness. If joy arises, then be exceedingly glad, for he has made you as his creation!

After you have experienced this practice, consider if there is a particular time or context where you find difficult emotions about your body arise (physical exercise, buying clothes, age milestones). Perhaps take these as an opportunity to do this practice again. How may you celebrate and thank God as you serve others in mission through your body?

Key Resources

- Psalm 139.

- Romans 12:1–2.

- Dallas Willard, *Renovation of the Heart: Putting on the Character of Christ* (NavPress, 2002). Chapter nine, "Transforming the Body," is a fascinating and critically important take on this topic.

Communion

Purpose
To see ourselves as part of the priesthood of all believers (1 Pet. 2:5) and to take seriously Jesus' invitation to participate in remembering his sacrifice and grace given freely to us.

Go Deeper
The story of the Last Supper is written in three of the four Gospels and 1 Corinthians 11. Technically, it was and is a meal. Historically, however, churches have turned this into a moment within our worship services, rather than a meal. We introduce communion as a practice here not to shun how it is commonly carried out today, but to instead grasp it and honor the depth of it within other contexts. Communion isn't just an act of individual remembrance; it was always designed as a practice for the *community* of God to share, together. It was a reminder that Jesus' body was broken for us, and his blood shed for us, but also that in Christ's act of sacrifice, we are invited collectively to be in union with him—and within the Trinity itself. This makes it very much a *communal* practice.

Jesus gives the disciples an invitation into his kingdom, and this invitation to participate is partly through the tangible practice of communion. Jesus told us to do this in true and holy remembrance of him (Luke 22:19; 1 Cor. 11:24). If we are in Christ, then we are part of a royal priesthood (1 Pet. 2:9), and we are therefore free to take communion in an informal setting.[1] For some of us who have been raised in more of a "high church" culture, where communion has solely been officiated by ordained clergy, this may feel particularly challenging. However, making the sacrament accessible should not make it less reverent or less spiritual but more so because it reflects the fact that our priestly office is only made possible because we can rest in the finished work of Christ. Our ability to take communion and to approach the throne of grace with confidence has nothing to do with our worthiness but Christ's (Heb. 4: 15–16).

There are some interesting theological differences across Christian denominations when it comes to the practice of communion. Roman Catholics view the Lord's Supper as an act of transubstantiation (Christ becomes the bread and wine); Lutherans view it as an act of consubstantiation (Christ's mystical and real presence with us in a unique manifest way); and the Zwinglian Memorialists view it simply as a ritual by which to remember Christ's sacrifice. Historically, these three views have been seen as divisive, but we propose pausing and considering the value of this historic debate. Whatever approach we take to the Lord's Supper, we must humbly recognize that many others have approached this differently throughout history. Perhaps we can learn from these other viewpoints, even if we do not agree with them.

As you engage with this practice, think about the billions of people who have done this in remembrance of Jesus since that first communion meal. Consider how you are a part of this expansive community that humbly comes before Jesus, who sacrificed his life—a community not only throughout the ages but also present now throughout the world. The body of Christ is united through this sacred meal that Jesus set in place. You are not alone in the celebration of this meal.

Missional Spirituality

Communion is a unifying practice as we are on mission alongside other believers. It reminds us of the good news we are inviting others to participate in. We can't welcome others to something if we are not

---

1   We also highly recommend taking communion regularly with others in the wider church family. This is often practiced differently from how we would take communion in our homes and can be an enriching experience, helping us to remember we are part of the wider body of Christ.

experiencing it ourselves. Communion helps us to remember and experience afresh God's incredible love for us. This, in turn, allows us to love others and call them to experience this amazing love as well. It also gives us confidence that we are not alone as we do God's kingdom work. In our Western culture, individualism is encouraged, and we can easily make faith a solely individual experience. This can lead to pride and disagreement with others while involved in mission. The Lord's Supper brings us back to our shared identity in Christ and reminds us his mission to the world is through a collective group of his people, not just individuals. We all share the same broken bread and the same cup (whether literally or metaphorically). No one has a greater claim to Christ's sacrifice, and therefore none of us have a separate claim to our kingdom work. Communion helps us remember we are working together, operating as one body, even if we represent different parts (1 Cor. 12).

Savor the Beauty

Jesus wanted something very tangible and simple to represent his body and blood, making this practice accessible to all who want to engage in it. Communion incorporates our whole beings and all our senses. As our whole beings enter into this experience, our hearts, minds, bodies, souls, and spirits are filled with thankfulness and nourishment. We are reminded who we are and to whom we belong. We are reawakened to the wonderful mystery of this new life we are invited into through Christ.

Practice

Take communion in private or with a friend! Grab wine (or juice) and bread (hearty and delicious bread is ideal!) and follow Jesus' lead in Matthew 26:26–29.

Allow yourself to enter this practice as a tangible way to use all your senses as you thankfully remember Jesus' sacrificial act that bestows grace upon you. Using your sight, look at the bread, observing its textures, colors, and shapes. As you break it, consider the particles of the bread being torn apart and the crumbs dropping as it is broken. Reflect on how this visual helps you understand Jesus' body broken for you. Then look into the deep red of the wine or juice. Think about how this reminds you of Jesus pouring out his blood for you. If you dip your bread into the wine, observe how the bread absorbs the wine into it. Give thanks to God for how he brought you into his family through his sacrifice. Smell the complex scents of the bread and the wine and allow this to whet your appetite. What memories do these smells convey? As you hear the words of Jesus spoken out loud, "Do this in remembrance of me," how does your spirit respond? Does your heart and head bow before this wonderful gift? Break the bread and feel its weight, its fluffiness, and its texture as you chew it. Consider how it nourishes your body and spirit. As you touch the cup and feel the liquid in your mouth, appreciate the satiating of your thirst, physically and spiritually. Finally, taste the complexity of the flavors both individually and mingled. Offer thanks to God for the gift of tasting and seeing that he truly is good. As your taste buds experience these flavors, you can be reminded that "God shows his love for us in that while we were still sinners, Christ died for us" (Rom. 5:8 ESV).

You might want to make communion more of a whole-meal practice by eating together with others in your Christian community. Perhaps you could plan a meal with others and take some time to share the Lord's Supper during the meal. This could be at the start, in between courses, or at the end. This practice is a reminder that the entire meal is part of being around the table with Jesus, joining in his invitation to commune with him and one another.

After you have experienced this practice, consider how you could explore different ways to practice communion, on your own and with those you meet regularly. Could you visit a different tradition of church to see how they practice communion? This can often engage your senses more as you are less familiar with the ritual in a different denomination.

_____

_____

_____

_____

_____

_____

_____

Key Resources

- Mark 14:22–25.

- John 13.

- 1 Corinthians 11:26.

- Marc Brown, "The Lord's Supper: Foundations and Practice in Puritan Liturgy," *Thinking About Worship*, December 17, 2018, https://thinkingaboutworship. wordpress.com/2018/12/17/the-lords-supper-foundations-and-practice-in-puritan-liturgy/.

- Ben Witherington III, *Making A Meal of It: Rethinking the Theology of the Lord's Supper* (Baylor University Press, 2007). This book is a vital rediscovery of the Lord's Supper based on historic insights into the early church and a plain reading of Scripture.

- You may also want to take on your own investigation into the historical dialogue between Martin Luther and Ulrich Zwingli regarding the Lord's Supper (see https://pursuingveritas.com/2014/07/15/luther-and-zwingli-on-the-lords-supper/ for an elementary entry point to the nature of their theological dialogue) or even further into the teachings of George Fox and the early Quaker church in response to this subject (see https://en.wikipedia.org/wiki/History_of_the_Quakers as a starting point). You will find that there is an immense range of views on this doctrine.

- You can discover various forms of modern liturgy for communion by searching online—or you could even have a go at writing your own.

Spiritual Friendship

Purpose

To reimagine and discover afresh the benefits and goodness of spiritual connections with others in the body of Christ.

Go Deeper

Not every Christian friendship is anointed or can be described as a spiritual friendship. In today's culture the term "friend" has been overused and often seems meaningless. Ironically, this word has been devalued by the use of social media, which allows us to be "friends" with someone we've never met or might not even speak to on the street. Yet to reclaim the value of true friendship we need a deeper awareness of love. C. S. Lewis said friendships begin when people realize they are not alone in their convictions or beliefs about something in the world—when they find someone else who comes alongside them and sees the world in the same unique way they do.[1] This unity and togetherness results in something more than mere companionship.

---

1   C. S. Lewis, *The Four Loves* (Harvest Books, 1971), 71.

A spiritual friend is one who walks with us through life and cares about our soul and spirit. More than simply spending time with us, a spiritual friend wants to know and be with us in the deeper things of this life, to savor Jesus together. Many reading this may realize they are starved of true spiritual friendship. If so, this is a good prompt to begin praying for or creating a spiritual friendship. Loneliness and isolation are significant problems in our culture, which means we have to be intentional in learning to serve others and point them toward deeper fellowship. Once we begin the journey of selflessness or self-forgetfulness and begin to elevate the glory and beauty of God as something worthy of all our attention and affection, we will start seeing others along the way who are walking the same path. We may even discover new friendships that were not so far away after all.

We may have experienced spiritual friendships that have faded away or fallen apart, and therefore this topic can bring up some sadness and grief. Because of this, we may be hesitant to enter this type of relationship again; we might put up walls to avoid getting hurt. If this is the case for you, try to bring your grief before God and ask him to bring healing and provide you the courage to enter a new friendship or press deeper into an existing one. Just because someone is gone from your life, it doesn't annul the good they invested and planted in you. It's all still part of you, and God has used it to make you who you are now. So don't let fear keep you from pursuing and deepening a spiritual friendship.

I (Jeremy) can attest to the power and goodness of a spiritual friendship. I have one spiritual friend in particular, Brandon, who has been a friend of mine since we were ten years old. We had our moments of weakness and even faded from friendship for a few of our teen years, but the Lord brought us back together in our twenties, and the friendship went deeper than ever. This time our friendship was based on our pursuit of Christ. We read Scriptures and pray together, and although we have other common areas of interest, it is Jesus that takes preeminence in our friendship. Over the years we have seen each other at our worst, yet we've always returned to the central core of our friendship: Jesus. We take an interest in the spiritual growth of one another, and we care about each other's interests, families, work, and well-being.

I also had the privilege of learning about spiritual friendship from some good role models. My dad had a lifelong spiritual friend, Greg, who felt like family to us all. Their friendship meant much to them, but it also meant much to the rest of us who watched it. We saw the effects of persistent, faithful friendship that bore fruit in Greg and my dad's lives. Greg became my friend too as I grew older.

If it wasn't for the model of faithful spiritual friendship I observed in my dad's life and then received myself through my friendship with Brandon, perhaps this concept would be harder for me to understand. But having had these experiences, I pray every follower of Jesus becomes attentive to the effects of loyal, honorable, and intentional relational deposits in the lives of others. Some friendships are appointed for only a season, so pay attention to any relationship that represents the overflow of the goodness of Jesus.

Missional Spirituality

Inevitably, spiritual friendships share a mutual understanding of the missional call of Jesus in each other's lives. Some of the best friendships are forged amidst a particular missional thrust or season of our lives, becoming even deeper because of this common task.

Jeremy and I have observed that sustainability in mission is usually linked to the existence of friendships and peers in the life of the missional practitioner. Church plants, ministry endeavors, and individuals often fail on the mission field because they lack enduring, healthy, and resourceful spiritual relationships. Spiritual friendships enable us to have a richer life, which causes a cascading effect of goodness in our other relationships and ministry.

We also believe spiritual friendships are foundational elements in most spiritual movements. Consider the movement Jesus started with the twelve disciples, the history of the Protestant Reformation with the early reformers who bonded together under a common vision, the Pentecostal movement who united around shared experience and vision, or the early Wesleyan/Methodist movement who found commonality in uniform practices and means of discipleship as they pioneered and took the gospel forward.

Savor the Beauty

Of course, we are invited into friendship with Jesus, the Father, and the Spirit. What we believe about this heavenly-spiritual relationship will impact how we conduct our earthly-spiritual relationships. God often uses others to demonstrate his love and goodness to us in more tangible ways. When we press toward a spiritual friendship, we are opening ourselves to see God's beauty reflected to us through this friend. When we are aware that God is our mutual friend in this spiritual friendship, we realize that as we laugh, he laughs with us. As we cry, he cries with us and wipes away our tears. He is with us.

Practice

Go out of your way to connect with one close spiritual friend. Who are the people in your life who are your closest friends and who also point you to Christ in significant ways? Consider your first impressions when you engage in fellowship; how do you feel? What does this relationship mean to you? How does it impact your faith? Investing in spiritual friendship can look like catching up over a coffee, walking together, doing an activity, or even engaging in mission together. It might also look like participating in spiritual practices together. Maybe you could invite a spiritual friend to join you as you grow in these spiritual practices.

After you have experienced this practice, consider how you can ensure you don't let the spiritual friendships you have slip away because you get too busy or lose touch. If you don't feel like you have any clear spiritual friendships at the moment, how could you invest time in getting to know others who might be those people? Where do you need to prioritize fun and deeper conversations with other Christians, rather than only focusing on missional tasks?

Key Resources

- John 17:20–23.
- Colossians 3:15–16.
- Hebrews 10:25.
- Larry Crabb, *The Safest Place on Earth: Where People Connect and Are Forever Changed* (W Publishing Group, 1999) and *Connecting: Healing Ourselves and Our Relationships* (Thomas Nelson, 2005).
- Hugh Halter and Matt Smay, *The Tangible Kingdom Primer* (Missio Publishing, 2009).
- Bill Hull, *The Complete Book of Discipleship: On Being and Making Followers of Christ* (NavPress, 2006).
- C. S. Lewis, *The Four Loves* (Harvest Books, 1971).
- James Bryan Smith, *The Good and Beautiful Community: Following the Spirit, Extending Grace, Demonstrating Love* (IVP, 2010).

Simplicity

Purpose

To learn to lessen our grip on material possessions and increase our margin for more time engaging with God and his kingdom. To learn to steward our energies and resources wisely with respect to our relationships, both with God and others.

Go Deeper

As intermediate rock climbers, Jeremy and I have found that on certain climbing routes the climber must exert all their energy to complete a move. Sometimes the difference between success and failure can be as little as 1–2 lbs of weight. There are moves where we can only get one or two fingers onto the next hold, and whether the climb is a success is determined by the strength of those fingers to carry just a couple more pounds of body weight. Think about that: an entire route can be contingent on one or two fingers handling an extra 1–2 lbs of pressure! (This pressure may not even be downward; it may be a sideways push.) As an athlete's finesse in any sport grows, minor amounts of friction or weight can have a significant impact on success. So it is in our spiritual lives too. Friction in this case often comes in the form of idols our hearts are grasping for. We need to throw off every weight that so easily prevents the climb and press on! What friction reduces our ability to connect with Jesus? What extra weight is stopping us from making that next move?

As followers of Jesus, we must take seriously the biblical exhortation to throw off everything that hinders us (Heb. 12:1). As we examine what is cluttering our lives, we should also look at the values underpinning our existence. Are we believing what our culture is telling us—what we should do or look like to be "successful"—or are we living out of kingdom values and believing who God is calling us to be? Often people try to do and be everything. But can we instead live out of an awareness of God's abundance toward us, his care and protection for us, and his ability to hold all time and accomplish all that must be accomplished? Often a mentality of scarcity produces clutter in our lives because we fear we won't have enough or be enough. When we realize God's loving abundance toward us, we can be at peace and not use other things as crutches to help us feel satisfied. This is a practice of realizing that more and bigger is not necessarily better. What can simple faithfulness grounded in a deep trust in God look like in our lives?

 ## Missional Spirituality

When he sent out the Seventy-Two in Luke 10, Jesus told the disciples to pack lightly. Not only did this ensure the disciples relied upon God for provision, but it also meant they had to rely more on those with whom they were sharing the good news. Jesus encouraged them to look for where they were welcomed and to stay with those people. Sometimes, when our lives are cluttered with our possessions and abilities, we miss the fact that God is bringing us to people who want to welcome us and are open to hearing the good news. Our material wealth and talents can inadvertently be what we offer to others, instead of pointing them toward what God wants to give them directly.

Simplicity is also helpful in making sure we are ready and flexible to respond to the priorities God has given us. Our ability to respond in an ongoing, sustainable way to the call of his mission will be influenced greatly by the clutter or lack of clutter in our lives. This is particularly important because it's so easy to allow the principles and values of our culture to mix with our kingdom principles.

Savor the Beauty

Although Monica and I don't have biological children of our own (though we do have many spiritual children), we love our friends' children, and every moment with them seems so precious. The same goes with a good friend or a spouse: we love and delight in this person! If there is friction or clutter in our lives that cuts back on our time with our loved ones, then we do what we can to reprioritize those valued relationships. The same goes for our walk with our Father. The trinitarian love God offers us is profound and is to be savored, studied, and internalized by the children of God. Let us take great care to remove any obstacles that hinder our fellowship with him.

Practice

Take some time to audit the clutter in your life. Clutter can be anything material, or things in your schedule or priorities that distract you from delighting in the Lord and responding to his missional call. Pick a few easy ones you can take care of today. Are there some practical ways you could simplify your life? You could clear out possessions to give away, make a meal plan and do food shopping for the whole week, "recycle" time by catching up with admin while on a journey, or prioritize people over perfection by spending less time on having a tidy home.

Next time you do this practice, go a bit deeper and think about some of the ways you may be allowing the influences of culture to impact your values and how you live.

After you have experienced this practice, consider how you can regularly purge distractions from your life. You may be surprised at how vital a regular rhythm this can be.

Key Resources

- Philippians 4:11–12.

- Hebrews 12.

- Mark Buchanan, *The Rest of God: Restoring Your Soul by Restoring Sabbath* (Thomas Nelson Inc., 2007).

- John Mark Comer, *The Ruthless Elimination of Hurry: How to Stay Emotionally Healthy and Spiritually Alive in the Chaos of the Modern World* (WaterBrook, 2019).

- Richard Foster, *Freedom of Simplicity: Finding Harmony in a Complex World* (HarperOne, 2005). See also his chapter on the topic in his book *Celebration of Discipline: The Path to Spiritual Growth* (Hodder & Stoughton, 2008).

- Richard Swenson, *Margin: Restoring Emotional, Physical, Financial, and Time Reserves to Overloaded Lives* (NavPress, 2004).

Although there are many new resources on minimalism (or essentialism) and it seems to be a bit of a fad, let's keep in mind that minimalism is not a fix-all. The historic goal of Christian simplicity is to remove obstacles to intimacy with the Father, Son, and Holy Spirit. You may still appreciate some of the insights that modern minimalists bring to the table; just read their writing with discernment. A few helpful secular voices on this topic include:

- Greg McKeown, *Essentialism: The Diligent Pursuit of Less* (Crown Business, 2014).

- Cal Newport, *Digital Minimalism: Choosing a Focused Life in a Noisy World* (Portfolio, 2019).

- Jenny Odell, *How to Do Nothing: Resisting the Attention Economy* (Melville House, 2021).

A Different Approach to Memorization

Purpose

To allow God's way of thinking to imprint itself on our way of thinking which, in turn, impacts our values and practices. To allow his words to become the words inside of us, and to allow his thoughts to become our thoughts.

Go Deeper

Many people struggle with Scripture memorization because they think of strict, rote repetition of verses. However, the key is to find a way to memorize Scripture that suits our personalities and preferences for learning. Some use music, some only memorize small portions, and some memorize large portions. Whatever the approach, the purpose is to experience the benefit of God's Word permeating our thoughts. When we memorize Scripture, it is like digging a well that is ready to be drawn upon for refreshment at other times. We might not always experience immediate transformation as we memorize Scripture, but we can draw upon it at other times, bringing us revitalization, peace, courage, or equipping when we need it. Scripture memorization yields fruit that arises at unexpected but necessary moments throughout our lives. It also imprints something from the mind and thoughts of God onto our minds, enabling us to be renewed specifically in our thinking patterns.

One way to change your approach to memorization is to learn an outline of a book of the Bible. Often people miss the big picture and logic behind entire books of Scripture. None of these books were mere collections of quotes randomly thrown together. (Even Proverbs has intentionality behind its flow.) The Spirit of God inspired human authors, and they purposefully crafted their arguments. Too often, under the guise of "digging deep," Christians spend copious amounts of time examining tiny details in one or two verses but miss out on the bigger picture. Focusing on the details and memorizing small portions is also beneficial, but seeing the big picture can transform our understanding of who God is and how he relates to his people. Some truths in Scripture are discovered via a magnifying glass; others must be seen with a bird's eye view. The same goes for memorization.

Missional Spirituality

Many times on mission, Jeremy and I have shared an outline of an entire book of the Bible with someone. Sometimes it was in an evangelistic setting, and other times it was in an equipping setting, where we encouraged a spiritual leader to keep perspective by remembering the macro-biblical points. There have also been times when the sheer knowledge of a full book of the Bible has greatly increased our faith during a difficult time. One time, we had a conversation with a friend where the entire conversation kept returning to the flow of the book of Acts. It struck us that perhaps the Lord was reminding us of his kingdom and mission work, not through specific verses but through a broader meta-narrative. Memorizing an outline of a biblical book is an incredible tool for the missional toolbelt.

Savor the Beauty

God inspired all the Scriptures, and his logic is evident throughout. To see the orderly mind of God is to see something unique about his character. Consider creation: when we study biology or chemistry, we see the order with which God creates. It is the same with the outlines of Scripture. Take Romans for example, an excellent book to study and memorize in outline form.

Imagine looking at a famous work of art. Sure, we can appreciate the details of the brushstrokes up close, but stepping back and seeing the grand picture makes all the difference. Try it out with the masterpiece of Scripture!

Practice

Start with an outline of one of the smaller books. You may want to use a study Bible, commentary, or an online outline for the particular book you have chosen. You may also want to study a book of the Bible and develop your own outline. Keep in mind that an outline is an interpretation; it is our attempt to see the patterns and order that the original author constructed, so there are many views on how an outline may unfold in a given book.

Example: Ephesians (a constitution for the church)
Here are a few outline examples for the book of Ephesians.

Simple:

- Chapters 1–3 (doctrine: our riches in Christ)
- Chapters 4–6 (application: our responsibilities in Christ)

In-depth:

- Chapter 1 (salvation doctrine of riches in Christ)
- Chapter 2 (salvation and unity)
- Chapter 3 (mystery of gospel and prayer)
- Chapter 4 (unity of the body, purpose of gifts, and body life in love)
- Chapter 5 (body life in love)
- Chapter 6 (spiritual warfare)

Watchman Nee's Outline:[1]

- Chapters 1–2 (sit)

---

1   See Watchman Nee, *Sit, Walk, Stand: The Process of Christian Maturity*, 4th ed. (CLC Publications, 2009). We quote this outline cautiously, for the writing of Watchman Nee requires discernment. But the outline is nonetheless helpful.

- Chapters 3–5 (walk)
- Chapter 6 (stand)

In note form, write down the outline of the book of the Bible you have chosen (similar to the Ephesians example above). You can make this as comprehensive or as simple as you want, but we recommend starting simple, so you easily retain the information. Try memorizing this outline and commit to recalling it, either verbally or in written form, each day for the next week. As you commit this outline to memory, ask God to give you fresh perspective and wisdom from him.

After you have experienced this practice, consider how this practice could become a useful tool to share with others in your mission context or Christian community.

Key Resources

- Psalms 119:11 and 97.

- 2 Peter 1:12–15.

- Michele Miner, *The Word of God: Unleashing the Power of Scripture Memorization* (CrossBooks, 2012).

- Donald S. Whitney, *Spiritual Disciplines for the Christian Life* (NavPress, 2014). Chapter two discusses memorization.

- The Bible Project, https://bibleproject.com/.

Prayer for Enemies

Purpose

To follow in the ways of Jesus and discover how to be filled with love rather than hate; and to find that goodness is better than contempt or anger.

Go Deeper

The psalms and prophets give us plenty of examples of God's people praying for justice and condemnation against their enemies. But Jesus taught the disciples to pray for the good of those who were against them (Luke 6:28). Jesus also demonstrated this through his life, right up until his death, when he asked for forgiveness for those murdering him (Luke 23:34). This isn't to say we shouldn't cry out for justice, but instead to show us the kingdom of heaven is a realm of mercy, love, and forgiveness. The importance of this practice has more to do with our internal condition and posture than the outward resolution of a situation. There will be times when we must seek justice, uphold boundaries, and create distance from our enemies; this is wisdom. But we can do the internal work of bringing our spirits and hearts to a place where we are not reinjured every time we think about those who have hurt us. The healing this practice brings helps to release us so we can, in wisdom, make the right decisions for our protection and the protection of others.

I (Jeremy) have known a few individuals who have done unspeakable evil toward me over the years. Though I used to long for justice, I began to pray for mercy instead. It felt like going against my natural way of thinking. But eventually it transformed me so that I genuinely wanted them to know God's love and have eternal life. I realized that those who had hurt me must have a miserable existence, since the things they had done would have also expanded their knowledge of evil itself. To do an act is to be changed by the doing of the act, so to do something deeply wicked is to allow wickedness to change us. But the same goes for righteousness and love. To do an act of love is to gain experiential knowledge of that love, and thereby to be changed by it. Praying for my enemies has caused me to desire they are delivered from their current state of darkness into the realm of light.

C. S. Lewis had a list of enemies he prayed for, including personal enemies as well as public enemies he didn't know personally but knew of their evil deeds. (Hitler and Stalin were on his enemy list, for example.) What if we prayed for public figures who outraged us? What if we prayed lovingly for their deliverance from darkness to light? What if we prayed so sincerely for Jesus to transform them, allowing his kindness to lead them to repentance? It would change our stress levels, it would put a halt to our gossiping lips, and it would eradicate the contempt we so easily hold within ourselves. I (Jeremy) can testify to this personally. In recent years, no one has made me more upset than Christians who tarnish the reputation of Jesus. But I began praying for them as if they were my enemies. As I did, Jesus gave me love for them. I've been set free from that anger, which could have led to contempt.

This prayer is not about bringing our complaints about other people to God. Often when we have taken offense or perceive someone to be our enemy, we don't see them accurately, but rather through a lens of deep pain and emotion. We must be careful to pray for them as image-bearers, created by God and capable of mind-boggling redemption. It may initially be hard to see them that way. But as we ask God to demonstrate himself and his love to them, we can stop seeking revenge or justice on our terms. This requires practice. Our hearts can trick us into believing our perception is the only right interpretation of that person. But praying for our enemies allows us to humbly acknowledge we don't know everything, and we surrender to the One who does. We will need to return to this practice regularly, as it seems there is always another offense we must forgive.

Missional Spirituality

On mission we will see the grave injustices in this world up close. We cannot fight them without supernatural power, otherwise we become drawn into a trap of human warfare. Our struggle is not against flesh and blood but against spiritual forces (Eph. 6:12), so we must be ready for our hearts to be supernaturally charged with God's love. We can bring more transformation to the communities to which we are called when our motives are fueled by love instead of hatred (1 Cor. 13:1–3). Praying for our enemies allows us to discover new ways to minister to them and bring the love of Jesus and the power of the gospel into their lives, even if it's through prayer alone. Praying for enemies opens our eyes to the real nature of the world around us. Contempt only blinds us and dulls his mission from our hearts.

Savor the Beauty

We also can become blind to the goodness and beauty of God if we walk with contempt toward others, or if we hold grudges. However, praying for our enemies reminds us that we ourselves were once enemies of God, but now he has forgiven us, and we are made to have peace with him, adopted into his family. This is the very nature of the gospel itself. Meditate on these verses:

And you, who once were alienated and hostile in mind, doing evil deeds, he has now reconciled in his body of flesh by his death, in order to present you holy and blameless and above reproach before him.

COLOSSIANS 1:21–22 ESV

"Alienated and hostile in mind" is written as "enemies" in some translations, but God reconciles us. What beauty to be savored in this truth.

But God shows his love for us in that while we were still sinners, Christ died for us. Since, therefore, we have now been justified by his blood, much more shall we be saved by him from the wrath of God. For if while we were enemies we were reconciled to God by the death of his Son, much more, now that we are reconciled, shall we be saved by his life. More than that, we also rejoice in God through our Lord Jesus Christ, through whom we have now received reconciliation.

ROMANS 5:8–11 ESV

Perhaps nothing puts it in better perspective than that. If we believe these verses are true for ourselves, and if we live in light of them, we will discover that praying for our enemies is one of the most supernaturally logical actions we can take, even if it doesn't seem natural to our earthly way of thinking.

Practice

Make a list of people who have been unkind or hurtful, or maybe people you simply can't stand, and then pray for them. Ask the Lord to transform them by his love, grace, and goodness and to transform you as you pray for them. This is not a time for an imprecatory prayer (for justice and punishment), but instead it is a time to pray for mercy on those you feel are enemies or antagonistic to your values. Keep in mind it doesn't have to be for someone you know; it could be a public or international figure that has offended you in some way or caused pain in your life.

This may seem like one of the hardest practices, but trust that as you practice this, Jesus will bring you strength and freedom.

After you have experienced this practice, consider how you could spend time praying for your enemies on a daily, weekly, or monthly basis. If this practice is particularly challenging because of harm you have experienced at the hands of others, with whom could you process that experience—a therapist, counselor, or trusted friend?

_____

_____

_____

_____

_____

_____

_____

_____

_____

Key Resources

- Matthew 5:44.

- Luke 6:27–28 and 23:34.

- Howard Thurman, *Jesus and the Disinherited* (Beacon Press, 1996). This was the book that Martin Luther King Jr. carried around with him and was profoundly inspired by. As a Black man in the early twentieth century, Thurman certainly experienced the horrors of racism. In this book he speaks directly to those who have been disinherited from the main culture around them and reveals how Jesus was disinherited in multiple ways. Thurman holds up Jesus as an example of forgiveness and then reveals from his own life how he also learned to love and forgive those who had hurt him.

- Miroslav Volf, *Free of Charge: Giving and Forgiving in a Culture Stripped of Grace* (Zondervan, 2006).

- Everett L. Worthington, Jr., *Steps to REACH Forgiveness and to Reconcile* (Pearson Learning Solutions, 2008) and *A Just Forgiveness: Responsible Healing Without Excusing Injustice* (IVP, 2012). Everett's personal story is one of the most staggering testimonies of forgiveness we have ever heard.

Forgiveness

Purpose
To discover the joy, goodness, and wonderful nature of forgiveness as part of the deeper healing and kingdom activity the Spirit desires to activate in each of our lives.

Go Deeper
Although the previous practice was oriented around praying for enemies, this one deals more with the heart issue of forgiveness. Both practices overlap, so Jeremy and I considered it vital to include them back-to-back. We realize some readers may be unable to legitimately follow through with the previous practice because there is too much pain to take those steps. It might have revealed a struggle in the area of forgiveness. In response, it is helpful for us to pause and consider the forgiveness the Lord has given us.

The biblical pattern for forgiveness always starts with the realization that we are forgiven by God. Ephesians 4:32 gives a reminder to "forgive each other just as God forgave you in Christ" (NCV). Christian forgiveness can't merely be a response to a moral command, an act of self-sacrifice, or an ignorant turning away from injustice;

rather, it must flow out of a response to the invitation God has given us, through his grace, to step into his love.

Some of us may find it hard to believe we are forgivable. But the Bible is clear that none of us are beyond God's forgiveness (Rom. 5:18). Our responsibility is to simply receive his forgiveness, recognizing that the God of the universe declares us righteous because of the work of Jesus. Nothing can change that. To assume we are unforgivable is to mistrust the truth and goodness of God or act as if the work of Jesus is not enough.

Jeremy and I have found that true forgiveness of others brings us to a place of *sympathy* toward those who have hurt us, then beyond sympathy to a place of willing *release* of our claim for revenge, then further to a place of *gratitude* for that person's life, then one final step to a place of praying *blessing* for that person.

To not forgive is to harm ourselves more than we can imagine. To hold onto unforgiveness is to allow the pain of the past to control us. On the other hand, to forgive is to take the offense and the offender before the Lord, to yield to his love, and to allow his love to show us the true nature of ourselves, our offenders, and our woundedness. Forgiveness starts with a choice rather than a feeling. If we based forgiveness on feelings, then it would rarely happen. But we have the choice to say, "Lord, help me forgive, and help me see how you have forgiven me." It can take courage, faith, and a desire to do the right thing rather than to hold onto unforgiveness, and it's often only *after* we have chosen to forgive that we feel a sense of love and peace.

Forgiveness is not the same as reconciliation. *Forgiveness* is primarily between us and God, even if it involves us and another person. We release to the Lord the person who has done something wrong. We realize we are not the ones who can judge and hold onto condemnation. Forgiveness is also an act of trust that God will be the one who brings ultimate justice, redemption, and wholeness to our lives and others (including those who have harmed us). If we can trust that our God will do what is right, we can release our claim on condemnation. *Reconciliation*, on the other hand, requires both parties to want forgiveness to happen. Sometimes reconciliation isn't possible because the person may already be deceased, or one person doesn't want to enter back into the relationship.

Missional Spirituality

The good news is a message of love, forgiveness, reconciliation, and life. If we remain in a place of believing we are unforgivable, or if we remain in a place of holding unforgiveness against others, we position ourselves against grace and goodness. By embracing the good news of God's love for us, and by extending that good news to others, we enter into his kingdom. When we forgive, we experience a healing that transforms us and helps us speak with others with a tone of mercy and grace. Those who allow Jesus to bring them to a place of peace and forgiveness reflect his light to the world around them. Our mission changes when we approach it as people who are both forgiven and forgiving.

Savor the Beauty

Forgiveness is a precious gift God gives us. We don't "earn" his forgiveness through our works, yet he delights to pour it out to us. Being a God who forgives and reconciles sets him apart from all others.

To both be forgiven and to forgive allows more light and goodness from Jesus to enter our lives. Jeremy's dad, Tom, spent many years as a counselor and saw people transform when they learned to follow Jesus into a place of forgiveness. "As deep as the wound goes is as deep as the healing can go," he used to say. "The deeper the wound, the deeper the healing that can be possible in Christ; the deeper the forgiveness, the deeper the healing."

Tom modeled this in his own life. Even though he experienced some terrible things others had done to him, he had been able to forgive them, and even in his final days on earth, he was still learning the beauty of forgiveness. The Lord always wants to bring us into deeper levels of forgiveness.

Practice

Spend some time prayerfully considering forgiveness. Start by reflecting on the forgiveness you have already received—or have yet to receive.

Read Luke 7:36–50 and prayerfully ask the Lord what it has looked like for him to forgive you. Do you find it easy to be thankful for that forgiveness? What is the impact of God's forgiveness on your life? In contrast to the Luke passage, you may also want to read Matthew 18:21–35. Do you know yourself as the servant who has been forgiven a huge debt? Can you forgive a smaller debt someone has against you?

Now focus your attention on those God may reveal to you whom you need to forgive. Write down a list of those God is highlighting to you. As you write their names down, ask God to help you see them with his eyes and to help you to want to forgive (especially if it feels difficult). Think about the heart Jesus had in saying, "Forgive them, for they know not what they do" (Luke 23:34 ESV). If you are experiencing blockers for you to forgive, write down these feelings and continue to offer them to God in prayer. Where do you need to know more of God's character so you can trust his justice and mercy for those you want to forgive?

After you have experienced this practice, consider how you can continue to grow in practicing forgiveness so you can be quick to forgive others (Col. 3:13). If you are struggling with forgiveness, where could you seek help to process your hurt and move toward freedom?

Key Resources

- Matthew 6:12–15.

- Ephesians 4:32.

- Colossians 3:13.

- Rusty Rustenbach, *A Guide for Listening and Inner-Healing Prayer: Meeting God in the Broken Places* (NavPress, 2011).

- Howard Thurman, *Jesus and the Disinherited* (Beacon Press, 1996).

- Miroslav Volf, *Free of Charge: Giving and Forgiving in a Culture Stripped of Grace* (Zondervan, 2006).

- Everett L. Worthington Jr., *A Just Forgiveness: Responsible Healing Without Excusing Injustice* (IVP, 2009) and *Steps to REACH Forgiveness and to Reconcile* (Pearson Learning Solutions, 2008).

- Flora Slosson Wuellner, *Prayer, Stress, and Our Inner Wounds* (Upper Room, 1998).

- William P. Young, *The Shack: Where Tragedy Confronts Eternity* (Windblown Media, 2007).[1]

---

1   Although we understand this is a controversial book, remember it is not to be taken literally. It is an allegory, and abstract thought and metaphor are not to be confused with concrete dogmatic claims. The full force of the book is concerning the love of the Trinity for us and is worth examination specifically when considering forgiveness.

The Beloved Charter

Purpose

To recognize and internalize God's deep love for us through creating our own written charter.

Go Deeper

There is no more powerful truth we must realize than the fact that we are loved—it changes everything. Creating a Beloved Charter involves writing down the key things God says about us so we can remind ourselves of his vast and ongoing love.[1]

God's love for us is trinitarian. *The Father* so desired that we be welcomed into his family as his beautiful children that he sent his own Son to die on a cross. Our Father, who is in heaven, who has the most highly glorified name in the history of all names, whose kingdom is expanding, whose will is flawless in all the universe, gave us what we need for our bodies and our souls—the Bread of Life—and forgives us from all our sin. He enables us to forgive others. He leads us into an endless

---

1   We are grateful to our friend Trevor Hudson for inspiring us with this practice. You can read more about this in his book *Discovering Our Spiritual Identity: Practices for God's Beloved*, rev. ed. (IVP, 2010).

procession of triumphant victory and delivers us from evil. *Jesus* loves us this much: he took on flesh and suffered so we may enjoy the wisdom, beauty, and goodness of God like never before. He opened life and light up to us while we were enemies and in darkness. *The Holy Spirit* comes and dares to indwell us and bring us into his fellowship and oneness with the Father and Son, inviting us into eternal glory. In other words, we are called to be participants in eternal glory and radiance. This love from the Trinity changes everything. We are more loved than we can fathom.

Missional Spirituality

This is our mission: love! To recognize and embrace his love, and then to let that love spill over onto everyone and everything around us. As we allow God's Spirit to fill us with his love, we will see others as they truly are, and we will have compassion, pity, and mercy on them—even to the point of loving our enemies. When we realize the love God has poured out to us, we can turn and see how he loves those around us. When we receive his love, we can truly know that our worth is found in God, and not in the eyes of others. This helps us to be self-forgetful and allows us to love others and express to them how deeply our God loves them as well.

Savor the Beauty

God really is love! Everything he has ever done or said emerges from the reality of him *being love*. In Ephesians 3:17–19, Paul says he longs for the church to be rooted and grounded in love, to have the strength to comprehend with all believers the fullest dimensions of God's love. He emphasizes that the love of Christ is so large it's beyond our comprehension (verse 19). So we can enjoy paying attention to God's massive love for us. We can notice how beautiful and majestic it is. We will spend an eternity unpacking the depths of his love.

Practice

Begin writing a list of Scriptures that speak about your true identity in Christ—all the things that God says are true about you. Find a few key ones that are most meaningful to you, then write out a Charter as if God was writing these things directly addressed to you. Think of a Charter as a *covenant* from the Lord to you, a summary of his promises of love.

Here is an example of Henri Nouwen's Beloved Charter:

> *I have called you by name, from the very beginning. You are mine and I am yours. You are my Beloved, on you my favor rests. I have molded you in the depths on the earth and knit you together in your mother's womb. I have carved you in the palms of my hands and hidden you in the shadow of my embrace. I look at you with infinite tenderness and care for you with care more intimate than that of a mother for her child. I have counted every hair on your head and guided you at every step. Wherever you go, I go with you, and wherever you rest, I keep watch. I will give you food that will satisfy all your hunger and drink that will quench all your thirst. I will not hide my face from you. You know me as your own as I know you as my own. You belong to me. … Nothing will ever separate you from my love.* [2]

After you have experienced this practice, consider how you can regularly allow its words to soak into your mind, heart, and soul as a powerful reminder of God's vast love for you.

---

2 "Creating a 'Beloved Charter,'" P2C Students, https://p2c.com/students/resources/creating-a-beloved-charter/.

Key Resources

- Psalm 139.

- John 15:9.

- Colossians 1:13–14.

- 1 John 3:2; 4:7–19.

- Neil T. Anderson, *Living Free in Christ: The Truth About Who You Are and How Christ Can Meet Your Deepest Needs* (Gospel Light Publications, 1993). This book is a meditation on thirty-six biblical aspects of our identity in Christ.

- Jonathan Edwards, *The Sermons of Jonathan Edwards: A Reader*, Wilson H. Kimnach, Kenneth P. Minkema, and Douglas A. Sweeney, eds. (Yale University Press, 1999). Specifically see last chapter, "Heaven is a World of Love."

- Trevor Hudson, *Discovering Our Spiritual Identity: Practices for God's Beloved* (IVP, 2010). Specifically his section on the "Beloved Charter."

An Energizing Cycle

Purpose

To continue benefiting from the spiritual practices we have engaged with in a sustainable and joy-filled way.

Go Deeper

If you've made it to this point in the book, then you have gone through quite a journey. Throughout these thirty-one days, we have flowed in and out of many themes, but they are all centered around the same principle: invest in intimacy with Jesus, walk with him, and experience more of his kingdom fruitfulness and joy as we partner with him on mission in this world.

As we reflect on all of the spiritual practices we have engaged with, we want to consider how we may fuel our ongoing journey, with these practices being a part of how we live missionally. The apostle Paul spoke of pressing on to attain the goal (Phil. 3:14), and we want to be those who persevere and know the prize of continued intimacy with God. But although it is good to have this focus, it is important for us to remember that Jesus' invitation to follow him isn't intended to be burdensome or something we strive for. Instead, he wants us to experience his rest and know that his yoke is easy (Matt. 11:28–30).

As we practice missional spirituality, we can discover Jesus' light and easy yoke when we focus on growing in the practices that come most naturally to us. The phrase "path of least resistance" is often used in a negative way to mean avoiding persevering through the challenges of life. However, imagine a fast-flowing river, rushing around rocks and boulders—the water flows most naturally and most quickly in the places where its path has already been cut around, rather than over, the rocks and elements standing in its way. So it is with us. As we lean into the practices we find most natural, we build momentum in our intimacy with God that starts to energize us to engage in practices we previously found to be more difficult.

This becomes a positive cycle: the more we invest time and energy into righteous living, walking by the Spirit, and savoring the Lord, the more we will want to continue doing so. If we try this by our own effort (as opposed to relying on his grace) then of course we will burn ourselves out! But if we allow his love to entice us and draw us in, we will want to continue following him into the good works he has prepared for us (Eph. 2:8–10).

We don't want to deny that it is worthwhile engaging with these spiritual practices even when they feel difficult; pain and discomfort can be connected to the process of laying down the idols we have put in place of God or letting go of untruths we have believed. But the more we practice identifying God and seeing his love and beauty, the easier we find it to respond to him and follow him more closely. It's not that we won't do hard things, but we will do them with joy because they are at the invitation of the Lord.

Missional Spirituality

Living a missional life based on our own strength is a great recipe for burnout. But if we instead listen to the Lord and pay attention to what he is doing, we will find the ways of life he is calling us into. What's more, our journey can benefit those we walk with in our missional contexts as we all have different ways of engaging with God that come more naturally to us. When we work together, each contributing our unique experience, we are more enriched by God's presence as a community of Jesus-followers. This is one of the reasons Monica and I encourage groups of people to use this book together!

Savor the Beauty

Once you taste something perfect, you won't forget it, and you will want more of this throughout your life—like Chicago deep-dish pizza or Costa Rican gallo pinto! The same is true of intimacy with Jesus. What is the most life-giving and beautiful encounter you have had with the Lord? How can you revisit that or replicate the actions that led you in that direction? This isn't about seeking a mere experience. It's about knowing God and drawing near to him, delighting in him as Psalm 37 commands us.

As you embark upon this ongoing cycle of growing in spiritual practices, consider this inverted haiku Jeremy wrote about going forward in our journey with the Lord:

Each New Horizon Attained

Opens a Few More

This is the Kingdom of God

Practice

Now that you have experienced each of the practices, consider which you would like to incorporate into your life on a more regular basis.

Think about the natural rhythms that would help you to do this: days, weeks, months, semesters, seasons, and years. Focus on the practices that are life-giving to you.

Throughout the thirty-one days, you have practiced acts of servanthood, acts of mission and visioning, acts of intimacy, acts of repentance and attentiveness, acts reinforcing the beauty of walking in holiness, acts conforming you to Jesus' image, and acts reminding you that you are more deeply loved than can possibly be measured. Ask yourself which practices provoked you the most. Which was easiest? Which was hardest? Which helped the most? Which helped the least? Where did you experience resistance? Which had more "payoff" than expected? Which of these practices may be worth investing more time and energy into? Which would you like to practice alongside others? Whom might you be able to learn from that finds other practices more natural to them? Where could you encourage and contribute to others with the practices you find most natural?

Some practices will feel like swimming upstream and are more challenging for you, and there is a time and place for those. Others will be like swimming downstream and are indicative of areas where quick learning and growth can take place. Press into the practices you sense the Lord calling you into. This will lead to an energizing, sustainable rhythm of missional spirituality.

Key Resources

- 2 Corinthians 2:14; 5:6–21.

- Philippians 3:7–14.

- Hebrews 12:1–3; 12–13.

- Randy Alcorn, *In Light of Eternity: Perspectives on Heaven* (WaterBrook, 1999).

- Jeremy and Monica Chambers, *Kingdom Contours: Empowering Everyday People With the Tools to Shape Kingdom Movements* (Missional Challenge, 2020). You may want to read this book and ask about ways the Lord may be calling you into his kingdom work. We designed the book with the intention of providing catalytic equipping for the person who is ready to get more involved.

- Stephen R. Covey, *The 7 Habits of Highly Effective People: Powerful Lessons in Personal Change* (Free Press, 2004). This book is about self-leadership and is vital wisdom for living life in such a way as to keep the end in mind.

- Darren Hardy, *The Compound Effect: Jumpstart Your Income, Your Life, Your Success* (Vanguard Press, 2012). Although this is not a Christian book, the point he makes is about the compound effect of all our habits and decisions. There is a principle here that applies to the Christian who is intentional about how they are approaching the fulfillment of the call the Lord has put on their life.

- Timothy Keller, *Every Good Endeavor: Connecting Your Work to God's Work* (Penguin Books, 2014).

- Crawford Loritts, *For a Time We Cannot See: Living Today In Light of Heaven* (Moody Publishers, 2005).

- Andy Stanley, *The Principle of the Path: How to Get from Where You Are to Where You Want to Be* (Thomas Nelson, 2011) and *Visioneering: Your Guide for Discovering and Maintaining Personal Vision* (Multnomah, 2005). A study of Nehemiah.

APPENDIX 1

Fifty-Two Weeks
of Missional Spirituality

In the experimental testing phase of these practices, we found that practitioners were taking two different approaches to this material, depending on the season of life they were in. Some needed to wade into the material and practices over a longer period of time (much longer than thirty-one days), while others felt that thirty-one days was perfect for creating a focused challenge. If you find yourself in a season of life where thirty-one days feels too rushed, then try soaking deep into these practices for an entire year of transformation. Below is a suggested flow of the weeks that you can follow. Instead of having a different practice every day, you will do one practice for an entire week. We have also added two additional elements: Sabbath weeks and Fruit weeks.

On Sabbath weeks the purpose is to create space for rest and recovery from the demands and pace of life, time for allowing the Lord to bring his deep peace into your life. During these weeks, you can choose a spiritual or biblical theme—such as love, joy, peace, hope, or wisdom—to be attentive to. (You may want to take a look at the additional appendix on "A Weekly Rhythm" for some inspiration.) The idea is not to add any particular practice into your day (unless there is a highly restorative practice you desire for that day) but instead to simply ponder and pay attention to anything the Lord may communicate to you around that theme. During these Sabbath weeks, you are aiming for something that looks different from your usual patterns and rhythms of life. You may not be able to change your entire schedule for the week, but you can intentionally incorporate the theme of rest and peace into your week. If helpful, you can use some of the practices mentioned throughout the book, like breath prayer or centering prayer, or a focus on simplicity as a means of supplementing your week with restorative elements. The main purpose of these Sabbath weeks is to make space so you can focus on doing things that restore your body, heart, soul, mind, and spirit. This may vary, according to your current needs. Sometimes you might want to be with people; other times you might want to spend more time alone. You may want to go on an adventure or stay home. You might want to cook a fun meal, or instead prepare enough food so you don't have to cook as often.

You may not be able to fully engage with rest that week, as work and family commitments continue, but the idea is to find rest in God as you trust in him with every aspect of your life. However, regardless of your season in life, we do highly recommend having one twenty-four-hour period of Sabbath. This allows us to experience a deep spiritual rest that we can take with us in our times of work and activity. It trains us to live from a place of rest, realizing we are not alone in our work because the Holy Spirit indwells us wherever we go.[1]

On Fruit weeks, allow the fruit of the Spirit that week (as listed below in the suggested plan) to be the theme. Be creative and look for ways to bring this into your daily life. Perhaps aim to daily bless someone with one of those fruits, or simply allow it to be your request each day that the Lord would draw you deeper into that fruit. You might want to do a study on the fruit to uncover deeper knowledge of how it can be present in your life.

For the rest of the weeks, simply read the corresponding chapters in the book and see how you can bring that practice into your weekly rhythm. Some practices may be easier to do "daily" for a week, while others may be better to do only once or twice within that week, depending on how much preparation and deliberation you want to add to your practice. You may want to use the practices more as a theme for your week, taking the principles of the practice with you even if you are not doing the whole practice every day.

Suggested Fifty-Two-Week Plan:

1. Journaling

2. Fasting and the Welcome Prayer

---

1 For a deeper dive into the spiritual aspects of Sabbath, *The Rest of God* by Mark Buchanan is perhaps the best book on the topic. Mark Buchanan, *The Rest of God: Restoring Your Soul by Restoring Sabbath* (Thomas Nelson Publishers, 2006).

3. Solitude and Silence

4. Sabbath 1

5. Fruit: Love

6. Praying Psalm 23 and the Lord's Prayer

7. Contemplative Prayer

8. Sabbath 2

9. Studying Scripture

10. Fruit: Joy

11. Soaking Prayer

12. Sabbath 3

13. Act of Kindness, Act of Generosity

14. Intercessory Prayer

15. Fruit: Peace

16. Sabbath 4

17. Practicing His Presence

18. Worship Music

19. Nature

20. Sabbath 5

21. Fruit: Patience

22. Praying the Hours

23. Gratitude

24. Sabbath 6

25. Immersion in Ecclesiastes

26. Fruit: Kindness

27. Modified Examen

28. Sabbath 7

29. Three Readings

30. Prayer of Recollection

31. Fruit: Goodness

APPENDIX 2

A Weekly Rhythm

Just as we have suggested a thirty-one-day or fifty-two-week journey, we have also found it helpful to try a weekly rhythm. If you enjoyed the thirty-one days or fifty-two weeks and want to try a new practice, then this is for you! Here you choose a "value" to focus on every day of the week and then repeat this for as many weeks as you like. These values can be things like love, joy, wisdom, vision, or practicing God's presence. I (Jeremy) have been doing this for several years and have even created some artwork that prompts me to remember my daily values. I also have notes reminding me to recenter on these values each day. The goal is to have a minimum of one touchpoint each day to focus on that day's values. If you're able, on some days you may want to orient the entirety of your day around the value. I find that on busy days I only have a few touchpoints, while at other times I center the flow of my day around a value. Below, I give a personal example of the values I try to remind myself of every week.

Sunday: Love
Monday: Rest
Tuesday: Joy
Wednesday: Union/Intimacy
Thursday: Vision
Friday: Wisdom
Saturday: Diligence/Craft

You can use different spiritual practices to focus on the value for the day. Here is a breakdown of how I take those values and add practices and particular Scriptures to meditate upon, but you can adapt as needed and select your own practices/values as you feel led.

Sunday: Love

- Meditate on 1 John 4 or 1 Corinthians 13.

- Reflect on the words: "We love because he first loved us" (1 John 4:19). Receive his love today, and express his love toward each person you meet. Practice the act of inclining your will toward others so that they may have what is best (perhaps as an act of secrecy).

- Read Jacob's request in Genesis 32:24–32. Pray the words modified from this passage as a breath prayer: "Bless me with your love, let me be transformed by your every provision."

- Spend time in contemplative prayer, considering John 14:23 where the beloved disciple leaned upon Jesus' chest. What would it be like for you to desire and express this same sort of intimacy with Jesus right now?[1]

- Finish the day with a night prayer, focusing on any key words that stood out from the passages above, for example, "But the greatest of these is love" (1 Cor. 13:13).

Monday: Rest

- Spend some time in soaking prayer, asking the Lord, "What do my soul, spirit, mind, heart, and body need today?"

- Meditate on this verse: "Come to me, all you who are weary and burdened, and I will give you rest. ... For my yoke is easy and my burden is light" (Matt. 11:28, 30).

- Use this request, inspired by various psalms, as a breath prayer throughout the day: "Restore my soul, revive my heart, bless me with your strength."

- Play worship music as you complete daily tasks.

---

1 John 13:23 tells us that a beloved disciple sat next to Jesus and laid his head on Jesus' chest. The assumption is that this was John, and they had such a close relationship they were able to engage in this powerful act of love. This inspires us to pray accordingly, that we might find our heads, metaphorically and spiritually, on Jesus' chest in rest and intimacy.

Tuesday: Joy

- Use the words "The joy of the Lord is my strength!" (Neh. 8:10) as a centering prayer throughout the day.

- Practice an act of kindness or generosity.

- Journal about all the things you can be grateful for, using the verse: "'The Lord is my portion,' says my soul, 'therefore I will hope in him'" (Lam. 3:24 ESV).

- Use the request: "Bless me, overwhelm me with your joy, unspeakable and full of glory" (adapted from 1 Peter 1:8).

Wednesday: Union/Intimacy

- Spend time in a contemplative practice, waiting on God's presence and paying attention to how you connect with him.

- Pray breath prayers throughout the day, inspired by the John 14 prayer "I am in you; you are in me."

- Memorize a verse about union with Christ.[2]

- Take communion.

Thursday: Vision

- Use the following requests as a way to pray the hours. Morning: "Let me gain Christ"; noon: "Let me forget what is past, and look ahead toward what is to come"; and night: "Let me press on toward the goal to win the prize." (See Phil. 1:21; 3:14).

- Spend time in scriptural study looking at Philippians 3.

- Spend time journaling, and think about the questions: how is Jesus calling me into his *missio Dei*? What excites me about this calling?

Friday: Wisdom

- Read Ecclesiastes.

- Spend time in soaking prayer, asking Christ to fill you with his wisdom, and meditating on Christ becoming "for us wisdom from God" (1 Cor. 1:30).

---

2   See https://www.openbible.info/topics/union_with_christ.

- Use this request, inspired by 1 Kings 3, as a breath prayer throughout the day: "Give me wisdom, give me Christ, and protect me from myself, by the power of your Holy Spirit."

- Spend time in spiritual friendship, for which seeking God's wisdom is encouraged.

Saturday: Diligence/Craft

- Spend time journaling and considering the question: "How can I hone my craft?"[3]

- Engage in the practice of presenting your body as a living sacrifice. Reflect on how your body allows you to use your skills and giftings for God.

- Use this prayer throughout the day: "And let the beauty of the Lord our God be upon us, And establish the work of our hands for us; Yes, establish the work of our hands" (Ps. 90:17 NKJV).

- Spend time in nature, contemplating God's own diligence and craft in creation.

---

3   "Craft" brings in the perspective that what we are doing for God is not just a job but has so many nuances that, when we see it as a craft, we will devote ourselves to training and growing in all its many facets. It implies a more life-encompassing posture with the work that God has called us to.

Acknowledgments

Over three hundred people have made an impact on this book. On the original blog we received feedback from hundreds of people who beta tested the thirty-one days. To all the peer editors and beta testers, thank you! To all our family, friends, professors, the people in Arise, Forge, Movement Leaders Collective, 100 Movements Publishing, The V3 Movement, and Renovaré, thank you! To all the authors who have influenced us (dead or alive), thank you!

Special thanks to the following:

Tyler and Kendra Yoder: our dear friends in Richmond, who gave us such clarity and added to our fortitude to keep going (even when we were tempted to give up on the project altogether). This book wouldn't have moved forward without the two of you.

Alan and Deb Hirsch: you have encouraged our writing at critical junctures, and we are grateful for your support and friendship over these years. Thank you also for generously writing the foreword.

Rowland Smith: thank you for supporting this work from the beginning and for enabling it to be done with excellence.

Brenna Varner: thank you for your friendship but also for your diligence in helping us with this entire process. (And thank you to you and Joel for the, hmm, very interesting TV show recommendations. We have now seen things we never thought could exist).

Anna Robinson: thank you for giving us major insight into our initial blind spots and helping this book come into being. Your insights and advice brought a level of health and vitality to this project; we are honored to have worked with you.

Helen Bearn: you are a miracle worker (aka, editor) who not only brought great clarity and congruence to the text but even provided helpful insight, dialogue, and content for the book. Helen, you are amazing; we were in tears of joy as we prayerfully thanked the Lord for your help on this project.

Uncle John: Rony.

Wendell Globig: thank you for all your help, dialogue, and support throughout this entire project.

Carolyn Arends: thank you for all your input along the way—our work with the Renovaré Institute gave us the opportunity to filter this entire project through the lens of what we were learning with Renovaré, and that in itself is priceless.

Father, Jesus, and Comforter: thank you, thank you, thank you.

Bibliography

Anselm, Saint (Archbishop of Canterbury). *Memorials of St. Anselm*. Edited by R. W. Southern and F. S. Schmitt O. S. B. Oxford: The Oxford University Press, 1991.

Aquinas, Thomas. *Aquinas' Summa Theologiae*. Edited by Stephen J. Loughlin. London: T & T Clark, 2010.

Augustine, et al. *The Works of Saint Augustine (4th Release)*. Charlottesville, VA: InteLex Corporation, 2014.

Avila de, Teresa. *Interior Castle*. Translated by E. Allison Peers. Mineola, NY: Dover Publications, 2007.

Boa, Kenneth. *Conformed to His Image: Biblical and Practical Approaches to Spiritual Formation*. Grand Rapids: Zondervan, 2001.

Bondi, Roberta C. *To Love as God Loves: Conversations with the Early Church*. Philadelphia: Fortress Press, 1987.

Buchanan, Mark. *The Rest of God: Restoring Your Soul by Restoring Sabbath*. Nashville: Thomas Nelson Publishers, 2006.

Byassee, Jason. *An Introduction to the Desert Fathers*. Eugene, OR: Cascade Books, 2007.

Calhoun, Adele. *Spiritual Disciplines Handbook: Practices That Transform Us*. Downers Grove: InterVarsity Press, 2005.

Calvin, John. *John Calvin: Selections from His Writings*. Translated by Elsie Anne McKee. Edited by Emilie Griffin. San Francisco: HarperSanFrancisco, 2006.

____. *Calvin: Institutes of the Christian Religion*. Edited by John T. McNeill. Louisville, KY: Westminster John Knox Press, 2011.

Chapman, Gary, and Jennifer Thomas. *The Five Languages of Apology*. Chicago: Northfield Publishing, 2006.

Chester, Tim. *A Meal with Jesus: Discovering Grace, Community, and Mission around the Table*. Wheaton: Crossway, 2011.

Clinton, Robert J. *The Making of a Leader: Recognizing the Lessons and Stages of Leadership Development*. Colorado Springs: NavPress, 2012.

Cloud, Henry, and John Townsend. *Boundaries: When to Say Yes, How to Say No to Take Control of Your Life*. Grand Rapids: Zondervan, 1992.

Coleman, Robert E. *The Master Plan of Evangelism*. Grand Rapids, MI: Fleming H. Revell Company, 1994.

Corbett, Steve, and Brian Fikkert. *When Helping Hurts: How to Alleviate Poverty Without Hurting the Poor... and Yourself*. Chicago: Moody Publishers, 2012.

Covey, Steven. *The 7 Habits of Highly Effective People: Powerful Lessons in Personal Change*. New York: Free Press, 2004.

Crabb, Larry, and Dan Allender. *Encouragement: The Unexpected Power of Building Others Up.* Grand Rapids: Zondervan, 2013.

Daley, Jerome. *Gravitas: The Monastic Rhythms of Healthy Leadership.* Colorado Springs: NavPress, 2020.

Edwards, Gene. *100 Days in the Secret Place: Classic Writings from Madame Guyon, François Fénelon, and Michael Molinos on the Deeper Christian Life.* Destiny Image, 2015.

Edwards, Jonathan. *The Works of Jonathan Edwards, Vol. 25: Sermons and Discourses, 1743–1758.* Edited by Wilson H. Kimnach. New Haven, CT: Yale University Press, 2007.

Elmer, Duane. *Cross-Cultural Servanthood: Serving the World in Christlike Humility.* Downers Grove: IVP Books, 2009.

Everts, Don, and Doug Schaupp. *I Once Was Lost: What Postmodern Skeptics Taught Us About Their Path to Jesus.* Downers Grove: IVP Books, 2008.

Fairbairn, Donald. *Life in the Trinity: An Introduction to Theology with the Help of the Church Fathers.* Downers Grove: IVP Academic, 2009.

Foster, Richard J. *Celebration of Discipline: The Path to Spiritual Growth.* San Francisco: Harper & Row, 1988.

____. *Prayer: Finding the Heart's True Home.* San Francisco: Harper Collins, 1992.

____. *Streams of Living Water: Essential Practices from the Six Great Traditions of Christian Faith.* San Francisco: HarperSanFrancisco, 2001.

Foster, Richard J., and Gayle D. Beebe. *Longing for God: Seven Paths of Christian Devotion.* Downers Grove: IVP Books, 2009.

Foster, Richard J., and James Bryan Smith. *Devotional Classics: Selected Readings for Individuals and Groups.* Rev. ed. New York: HarperOne, 2005.

Fraser, Robert. *Marketplace Christianity: Discovering the Kingdom Purpose of the Marketplace.* Overland Park: New Grid Books, 2011.

Gallagher, Timothy M. *The Examen Prayer: Ignatian Wisdom for Our Lives Today.* New York: Crossroad Publishing Company, 2006.

Gladwell, Malcolm. *The Tipping Point: How Little Things Can Make a Big Difference.* New York: Little, Brown and Company, 2000.

Guyon, Jeanne Marie Bouvier de La Motte. *Jeanne Guyon: Selected Writings.* Translated by Dianne Guenin-Lelle and Ronney Mourad. Mahwah, NJ: Paulist Press, 2012.

Hagberg, Janet O. and Robert A. Guelich. *The Critical Journey: Stages in the Life of Faith.* Salem: Sheffield Publishing Company, 2005.

Hagerty, Sara. *Unseen: The Gift of Being Hidden in a World That Loves to Be Noticed.* Grand Rapids: Zondervan, 2017.

Halter, Hugh, and Matt Smay. *The Tangible Kingdom Primer.* Littleton: Mission Publishing, 2009.

Hardy, Darren. *The Compound Effect: Jumpstart Your Income, Your Life, Your Success.* New York: Vanguard Press, 2010.

Hirsch, Alan. *Disciplism: Reimagining Evangelism Through the Lens of Discipleship.* Exponential Resources, 2014. Retrieved from https://exponential.org/resource-ebooks/disciplism/.

____. *The Forgotten Ways: Reactivating Apostolic Movements.* Grand Rapids: Brazos Press, 2016.

Hirsch, Alan, and Tim Catchim. *The Permanent Revolution: Apostolic Imagination and Practice for the 21ˢᵗ Century Church.* San Francisco: Jossey-Bass, 2012.

Hudson, Trevor. *Discovering Our Spiritual Identity: Practices for God's Beloved.* Rev. ed. Downers Grove: IVP, 2010.

____. *Holy Spirit Here and Now.* Nashville: The Upper Room, 2013.

Hull, Bill. *The Complete Book of Discipleship: On Being and Making Followers of Christ.* Colorado Springs: NavPress, 2006.

Hunter, George C. *The Celtic Way of Evangelism: How Christianity Can Reach the West ... Again.* 10th anniversary ed. Nashville: Abingdon Press, 2010.

Julian Of Norwich. The *Revelations of Divine Love of Julian of Norwich.* Translated by James Walsh. Trabuco Canyon, CA: Source Books, 1961.

Kalinowski, Caesar. *The Gospel Primer.* Littleton: Missio Publishing, 2013.

____. *Small Is Big, Slow Is Fast: Living and Leading Your Family and Community on God's Mission.* Grand Rapids: Zondervan, 2014.

Keller, Timothy. *Center Church: Doing Balanced, Gospel-Centered Ministry in Your City.* Grand Rapids: Zondervan, 2012.

____. *The Freedom of Self-Forgetfulness: The Path to True Christian Joy.* La Grange: 10Publishing, 2012.

Kelly, Thomas. *A Testament of Devotion.* San Francisco: HarperCollins, 1969.

Laubach, Frank C. *Letters by a Modern Mystic.* Edited by Gina Brandon and Karen Friesen. Colorado Springs: Purposeful Design Publications, 2007.

Lawrence, Brother. *The Practice of the Presence of God.* Translated by John J. Delaney. New York: Image Books, 1977.

Lawson, James Gilchrist. *Deeper Experiences of Famous Christians.* Anderson, IN: Warner Press, 2007.

Lewis, C.S. *The Great Divorce.* New York: Simon & Schuster, 1996.

____. *The Screwtape Letters.* New York: HarperOne, 2015.

____. *The Four Loves.* New York: HarperOne, 2017.

Loritts, Crawford W. *Leadership as an Identity: The Four Traits of Those Who Wield Lasting Influence.* Chicago: Moody Publishers, 2009.

McKelvey, Douglas Kaine. *Every Moment Holy, Volume 1.* Edited by Pete Peterson. Nashville: Rabbit Room Press, 2019.

Moon, Gary W. *Apprenticeship with Jesus: Learning to Live Like the Master.* Grand Rapids: Baker Books, 2009.

Nouwen, Henri J. M. *In the Name of Jesus: Reflections on Christian Leadership.* New York: Crossroad Publishing Company, 1992.

O'Donnell, James J. *Augustine Confessions: Volume 1: Introduction and Text.* Oxford: Oxford University Press, 2013.

Packer, J. I. *Evangelism and the Sovereignty of God.* Downers Grove: IVP, 2012.

Peterson, Eugene H. *The Contemplative Pastor: Returning to the Art of Spiritual Direction.* Grand Rapids: Eerdmans Publishing, 1993.

Russell, William R. *Martin Luther's Basic Theological Writings.* 3rd. ed. Edited by Timothy F. Lull. Minneapolis: Fortress Press, 2012.

Sande, Ken. *The Peacemaker: A Biblical Guide to Resolving Personal Conflict.* Grand Rapids: Baker Books, 2004.

Smith, James Bryan. *The Good and Beautiful God: Falling in Love with the God Jesus Knows.* Downers Grove: IVP, 2009.

Stearns, Richard. *The Hole in Our Gospel: The Answer That Changed My Life and Might Just Change the World.* Nashville: Thomas Nelson, 2014.

Taylor, Hudson J. *J. Hudson Taylor: An Autobiography.* Seattle: ReadAClassic.com, 2010.

Thomas, Gary. *Sacred Pathways: Discover Your Soul's Path to God.* Grand Rapids: Zondervan, 2000.

Thurman, Howard. *Jesus and the Disinherited.* Boston: Beacon Press, 1996.

Tucker, Ruth A. *From Jerusalem to Irian Jaya: A Biographical History of Christian Missions.* 2nd ed. Grand Rapids: Zondervan Academic, 2004.

Vanhoozer, Kevin J., Charles A. Anderson, and Michael J. Sleasman, eds. *Everyday Theology: How to Read Cultural Texts and Interpret Trends.* Grand Rapids: Baker Academic, 2007.

Ward, Benedicta, ed. *The Desert Fathers: Sayings of the Early Christian Monks.* London: Penguin Classics, 2003.

Warren, Tish Harrison. *Liturgy of the Ordinary: Sacred Practices in Everyday Life.* Downers Grove: IVP, 2016.

Watson, Thomas. *The Complete Works of Thomas Watson (1556-1592).* Edited by Dana F. Sutton. Lewiston, NY: Edwin Mellen Press, 1997.

Willard, Dallas. *Hearing God: Developing a Conversational Relationship with God.* Downers Grove: IVP, 1999.

____. *Renovation of the Heart: Putting on the Character of Christ.* Colorado Springs: NavPress, 2002.

_____. *The Divine Conspiracy: Rediscovering Our Hidden Life in God*. New York: Harper Collins, 1998.

_____. "The Kingdom of God: Teaching Series." (audio) Taped in 1990 at Hollywood Presbyterian Church. Audio.

_____. *The Spirit of the Disciplines: Understanding How God Changes Lives*. San Francisco: HarperCollins, 1991.

Wimber, John, and Kevin Springer. *Power Evangelism*. Bloomington: Chosen Books, 1986.

Woodward, JR. *Creating a Missional Culture: Equipping the Church for the Sake of the World*. Downers Grove: IVP, 2012.

Woodward, JR, and Dan White Jr. *The Church as Movement: Starting and Sustaining Missional-Incarnational Communities*. Downers Grove: IVP, 2016.

Made in United States
Orlando, FL
03 July 2024

48583536R00122